AFRIKANERS OF THE KALAHARI
White Minority in a Black State

T0371054

BOOKS IN THIS SERIES

AFRIKANERS OF THE KALAHARI

White Minority in a Black State

MARGO and MARTIN RUSSELL

CAMBRIDGE UNIVERSITY PRESS

CAMBRIDGE

LONDON·NEW YORK·MELBOURNE

CAMBRIDGE UNIVERSITY PRESS

Cambridge, New York, Melbourne, Madrid, Cape Town, Singapore, São Paulo, Delhi

Cambridge University Press
The Edinburgh Building, Cambridge CB2 8RU, UK

Published in the United States of America by Cambridge University Press, New York

www.cambridge.org
Information on this title: www.cambridge.org/9780521218979

First published 1979
This digitally printed version 2008

A catalogue record for this publication is available from the British Library

Library of Congress Cataloguing in Publication data
Russell, Margo J
Afrikaners of the Kalahari.
(African studies series; 24)
Bibliography: p.
Includes index.
1. Boers – Botswana – Ghanzi (District) 2. Ghanzi,
Botswana (District) – Social conditions. 3. Ghanzi,
Botswana (District) – Economic conditions. 4. Ethnol-
ogy – Botswana – Ghanzi (District) 5. Ghanzi, Botswana
(District) – Race relations. 6. Boers – Kalahari
Desert. 7. Kalahari Desert – Race relations.
I. Russell, Martin, 1929–   joint author. II. Title.
III. Series.
DT803.G48R87   309'.1'681   77–85693

ISBN 978-0-521-21897-9 hardback
ISBN 978-0-521-10140-0 paperback

Contents

Illustrations

Acknowledgements

Acknowledgements are due to the Social Science Research Council whose grant made the research possible; to the British Academy whose token support was most encouraging; to Archives de Sciences Sociales des Religions for permission to use Chapter 7; to our brother-in-law Peter Hill for easing the problem of transport in the Kalahari; to Robert Whyte for generously providing us with a house in the Kalahari; to various officials of the Government of Botswana for their ready cooperation at all times; to the people of Ghanzi, boer, Bushman and black, for their tolerant hospitality and memorable reminiscences, especially to the daughters of Jan Burger.

A note on terminology

The issue of what are the proper terms for the various ethnic groups in a plural society is a vexed one, since local attitudes towards the less powerful and less privileged groups rapidly reduce any appellation to a perceived perjorative. A common solution is to adopt a term used by some group other than one's own, thereby freeing oneself from the burden of cumulated contempt. Thus the editors of *The Oxford history of South Africa* chose to call Bushmen *San*, the term by which they were known to Hottentots, or *Khoi*, whose subject people they were from time to time. The Botswana government at first called the Bushmen by the English *Bushmen*, rather than the Tswana *Masarwa*, but have now settled for the Kgalagari *Basarwa*.

Place names can carry a similar emotional charge. We have used both *Namibia* and *South West Africa*, loosely guided by context. Ghanzi itself officially became *Gantsi* in 1973, but has since reverted. The historical record shows Khanzi, Chanse, Ghanzé, *inter alia*.

Bushman language groups introduce an additional complication. Not only does each language have its own terms for each group, but the words themselves challenge the limits of our alphabet by introducing an unusual range of sounds, upon the representation of which there is not yet any firm agreement. We have reluctantly contributed to the growing consensus by adopting the mystifying orthography /, //, ≠, !, of Barnard (1975), Silberbauer (1965) and others; we would have preferred the well-established Zulu and Xhosa notation for clicks.

We have followed A. Kuper (1970) rather than Schapera and van der Merwe (1943, 1945) in using *Kgalagari* rather than *Bakgalagadi*, since it has the advantage of making clear the connection between the people and the place. We have forsaken consistency in using *Tswana* rather than *Batswana*, but *Batawana*, *Bamangwato* etc. for the constituent Tswana tribes.

Because we have drawn liberally upon the transcript of tape-recorded conversations made in the Kalahari, inconsistency in terminology has been unavoidable. The following list of synonyms may eliminate confusion:

Damara = Herero
Hotnot = Hottentot = Khoi = Nama
African = Bantu = black = kaffir
Batswana = Bechuana = Motswana = Tswana

Currency presents a problem. We have not attempted to convert sums into contemporary monetary equivalents or familiar currencies. Before 1975 Botswana shared South African currency, £sd, until the introduction of the rand in 1961 when R1 equalled £0.5. In 1975 Botswana adopted its own currency, the pula, with P1 equalling R1 until 1976 when the pula was revalued 5 per cent.

We have retained the colloquial (Dutch) land measure, morgen, about two acres or 0.85 hectares. The typical Ghanzi farm unit of 5000 morgen is 4250 hectares.

We have changed the names of living people and their farms to preserve their anonymity.

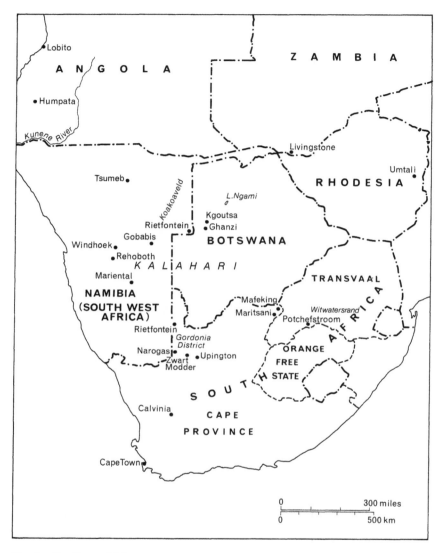

Fig. 1. Southern Africa

1

The mundane Kalahari: an introduction

In the public imagination the Kalahari is associated with Bushmen, and rightly so, since not only are they its majority group, but it is the only place where their hunting and gathering life style survives. It is the Bushmen who draw anthropologists and linguists by the score into the Kalahari.[1] This book, however, is about another Kalahari people, white Afrikaans-speaking cattle pastoralists who for three generations have occupied the limestone ridge in the western Kalahari that stretches from Gobabis in Namibia to the Kwebe Hills below Lake Ngami in Botswana.

Although these Afrikaners feature in the anthropological texts, they tend to be confined to the small type of footnotes or acknowledgements, shadowy subsidiaries, supplying petrol, acting as guides, interpreters and drivers, cited by name and occupation rather than collectively, since they spoil the stereotype of Afrikaners as the Bushman enemy and exploiter.[2] Perhaps they spoil the anthropological idyll. The anthropologists like to reserve to themselves the monopoly of intimacy with this anachronistic stone-age culture. The reality of the Kalahari is less romantic but in many ways more interesting.

Besides the Bushmen and the Afrikaners there are the various pastoral people who have been attracted to the remote empty grasslands: Coloured settlers from the northern Cape, Kgalagari from the south and west, Herero fleeing east from German rule in Namibia, and Barolong moving westwards to escape British colonial taxation. Then there are exotic individuals of all kinds: Hambukushu and Makuba from the northern swamps, Baster, Reheboth and Nama from the south, besides Bakwena, Bangwaketse and Bamangwato from the east and Americans, Danes and other European temporary sojourners, seconded to the administration under various aid and development programmes.

The administrative headquarters of this part of the Kalahari is known as Ghanzi Camp, a barren sun-blasted commonage on the limestone ridge. Seen from the ground the ridge is a very subtle topographical feature. It is true that the treacherously sandy tracks, which have splayed

Fig. 2. An Afrikaner and his wife: farmer, transport rider, guide and interpreter for American anthropological expeditions to the Bushman

confusingly yet monotonously for 650 kilometres through the flat Kalahari, rise and fall and rise again as one approaches the Camp, but the undulations are slight and one has little sense of having arrived at last on firm high ground, save for the litter of white limestone strewn beside the road now suddenly reassuringly hard and corrugated. The Kalahari vegetation persists – low, grey, brittle bushes, occasional tall trees with bright lime-green leaves, shiny brown or white seed pods, and delicate white thorns. The noticeable contrast is in the grass: the tall, blanched clusters, so frequent in the Kalahari and preserved on most of the cattle ranches that stretch for more than eighty kilometres on either side of the Camp, disappear, giving way to hoof-pocked, wind-blown, fine dry sand between stunted, colourless bushes, stripped by goats and the winter season of all foliage.

Here are the post office, the police station, the court house, the veterinary offices and the District Commissioner's office of the Republic of Botswana, which in 1966 became independent of the British protection it had been afforded for the previous eighty years. On wooden benches on the office verandah people sit, waiting to ask official permission to dig wells, to graze cattle on the commonage, to move cattle out of the district, and other matters of bureaucratic concern. As they sit they look out over the tidy squares of brittle lawn, carefully edged with stones, to the sandy road along which pass occasional grinding, high-wheeled cattle trucks and donkeys and mules, in teams pulling carts, or singly bearing serious adult travellers or laughing, racing children. This is the main road from Namibia to Ngamiland.

The constant flux of people testifies that this is indeed the capital of the area. The senior officials from eastern Botswana who step out of small chartered aircraft onto the rough landing strip behind the offices have an air of authority and a casual, self-conscious sophistication. This is their territory, yet they are outsiders; a term of duty in Ghanzi is a term of exile from the east, from one's own kind; it is to be plunged into a curious rural cosmopolitanism, administering the affairs of a host of Botswana's ethnic and cultural minorities. Locally recruited Kgalagari clerks wander between offices clutching files symbolising their status, and shouting amicably to one another and to friends passing by.

A hundred metres down the road is the local hotel, the Kalahari Arms, where administrators, cattle speculators and local farmers, black and white, sit on the cool verandah to drink and deal and speculate. Below them, at the hotel gate, Bushman children wait patiently with bundles of bows and arrows to sell to the occasional truck-load of tourists on safari. Until 1964 the verandah, bar and lounge had been the preserve of whites only, and on Saturday nights British officials and farmers had danced till the proprietor had banged the piano down and ordered them home. Independence has changed all that. The Saturday night dance at the hotel is not in the idiom of the new black administrators or their earnest overseas assistants as it was of the last of the British. Nor is the sale of liquor now restricted to the elite as in Protectorate days. Bushmen and Kgalagari flow in a ceaseless stream to the off-licence. Though the drink is new, the traditional drinking patterns and partners are preferred to the polyglot company of the hotel bar.

From the hotel verandah you can see the health clinic which, with its one doctor first appointed in 1973, and several nurses, a pharmacist and others, represents the official medical service to the district. The Ghanzi response to Western medicine displays all the caution due to an ill-tried innovation. Kgalagari and Bushmen retain their faith in the longer-established Bushman healing trance, choosing to spend as much as a month's cash wages on the divination services of a reputable Bushman

3

healer rather than the statutory sixty cents for treatment at the clinic. The Afrikaners too have developed an attitude to the treatment of ill health which cannot depend on the Western expert. 'In the old days, if you were sick and set out for a doctor, by the time you got there you were either better or dead.'[3] Each family has its medicine box stocked with a range of traditional herbal and chemical cures, most of them now patented, pre-packed in little glass bottles with cork stoppers, marketed from South Africa. Nowadays penicillin enters the boer repertoire along with bitter aloes, *rooipoeier* and *Hoffmansdruppels*.[4] Self-reliant in the treatment of most disorders, they are intensely interested in medicines and remedies and their comparative effectiveness. The word *dokter* is a verb rather than a noun among them. 'I know how to doctor', a woman will say. 'My mother taught me. She was very clever at it. All the people used to come to her.'

Opposite the clinic is a small settlement of hastily contrived temporary huts of sticks, newspapers, cardboard and flattened tins. Here Herero outpatients and their supporters ingeniously provide their own accommodation during treatment. On the sand between the makeshift huts the Herero women move like butterflies, their frilled and tiered brightly coloured cotton dresses sweeping the dun sand majestically. The dress, with distinctive headdress and small apron, is a nineteenth-century Finnish missionary legacy. Each takes fifteen yards of fabric, and the Herero customer is fastidious about quality. 'Only the best will do for them', says the Afrikaans woman who owns one of the three Camp trading stores. 'They're very good customers.'

The stores are treasure troves of every commodity for which there is black demand. From their rafters hang storm lanterns, strings of shoes, buckets, plastic bottles and horse saddles. On the shelves are blankets, shirts, trousers, dress materials, crockery, cutlery, patent medicines, sweets, tobacco and tinned foods. Once a week on Fridays great dusty trucks thunder in from across the Kalahari to replenish the stock and to bring a little fresh produce – bread, fruit, vegetables – demanded by the small dependent community of resident officials. Longer-established residents secure their own stocks of fresh food. The Afrikaans cattle ranchers bypass the trading stores altogether, buying in bulk directly, and supplying the transport upon which the stores rely. Nevertheless the store is for them too a focus of social life. Since the proprietors or managers are kinsmen, people passing by call in to lean on the counter and drink incessant cups of tea, amidst the babble of Nharo, Makoko, G/wi,[5] Herero, Kgalagari and Tswana customers. Extensive credit is extended to all through a system of mental account keeping. For despite its polyethnic character this is a small and intimate community and there are few people who are not known by face or name to most.

4

Fig. 3. The Oasis Cash Store. One of the three trading stores in Ghanzi Camp

Behind the administrative buildings is the compound of officials' houses, whitewashed concrete slabs shaded by cultivated trees planted years before by colonial officials. Here too is the Tswana medium primary school. It has not been open long. For years the building stood disused after the withdrawal of the Afrikaner pupils and teachers from the school following the abrupt British switch to racially integrated education in 1964.

On a windy day the fine sand blows off the roads and the veld, stinging the legs and obscuring in a thick pink haze the scattered houses of the Kgalagari and Bushman townsmen on the commonage. Bushman houses, even in the town, are frail affairs of sticks and dried grass, roofless in winter to facilitate large fires. Compared to the elaborate mud and clay architecture of the east, Kgalagari houses also are slight, slipshod and impermanent. The careful tight thatching of the east gives way to casual untidy bunches of grass loosely tied to the rafters, giving the dwellings a surprised air like the tousled hair of children suddenly awoken from sleep. The sudden whirlwinds that come spinning across the sand send the hens scuttling, set children shouting and make the old women suck their teeth in mild irritation. There is a noise like the crackle of fire as the dried leaves of past summer are flung against the dry branches of the bushes, and the loose thatch, empty cans and bits of cardboard are momentarily

5

funnelled into the vortex. The whites' houses also show a casual disregard for the niceties of structure and insulation which a harsher climate might demand. An unexpected wind in 1972 took off six roofs.

> The first week it came from one side and took off half the roof, and a week later it came from the other side; we hung onto the roof that night. For twelve hours we hung onto the beams and when the wind began to drop we got wire and fastened it down onto the lintels. I told my husband if he ever builds another house he must put walls on the roof to keep it down.

In 1972 there were 265 households, or a thousand people, living on the fifteen square kilometres of Ghanzi Camp.[6] A few of these were white Afrikaner traders, mechanics and their families. A substantial 43 per cent were the households of civil servants living in government houses. The civil service is mainly Tswana. An interesting index of the Africanisation of the civil service is the fact that in 1972 a third of Ghanzi officials owned cattle. Apart from a few Hereros and Coloureds, the remaining households were Kgalagari and Bushman, most of whom owned no cattle, nor received cash wages from any source. How they subsist remains obscure in the congested barren Camp, though in broad outline the pattern of no cattle, no cash is typical of most of Botswana, where seasonal crop cultivation and the use of borrowed cattle provide a subsistence base.[7]

TABLE 1. *Income of households living in Ghanzi Camp, 1972*

Source of cash income	Without cattle		With cattle		Total	
	No.	%	No.	%	No.	%
In government service	79	30	35	13	114	43
Non-government paid employment	37	14	8	3	45	17
No cash wage	83	31	23	9	106	40
TOTAL	199	75	66	25	265	100

Source: Ghanzi Commonage Survey (1972)

In some years the Camp fills with Bushmen, pressing in during the dry, barren winter months to find water. There are several boreholes in the Camp where water is found at eight metres. The galvanised iron windpumps dominate the skyline, and on a windy day careless disregard to disconnect the pump can rapidly result in water being splashed and spilled in the sand. Such a pump was seen by a poor white visitor from the northern Cape in 1952. 'I said to myself, if it's the kind of place you can waste water like that, it's the place for me.'

It seems paradoxical that anybody should have been attracted to Ghanzi by abundant water. To the outsider, Ghanzi appears to be more of a desert than the rest of the Kalahari. Yet this very barrenness has been brought about by the water which allows people and stock to congregate, in turn rapidly reducing the veld to sandy waste. It was the availability of water on the limestone ridge which first attracted the white Afrikaner settlement there in 1898, when forty-one families were allocated 5000 morgen each[8] under the patronage of Cecil Rhodes. Eighty years later the Afrikaans community is still less than fifty families strong, but their farms stretch for more than a hundred and fifty kilometres along the ridge.

The intervening years have seen a number of changes in the size and strength of the Afrikaner community and its economic and political circumstances, but none more dramatic than their encapsulation into the independent state of Botswana in 1966 when the British relinquished their Protectorate in Bechuanaland.

All our preconceptions of Afrikaner political and racial attitudes sensitised us to the potential impact of the advent of black majority rule for the white community of Ghanzi. In their reaction we hoped to find portents for the process of change in southern Africa as well as grist for the mills of sociological theories of race relations.

Most studies of blacks and whites have been of rich whites and poor blacks, or powerful whites and powerless blacks. This is the colonial heritage. It is particularly true of Africa. Even where whites have been deprived of political power they have generally retained sufficient economic influence to make formal loss of political power unimportant, at least in the short run. The Afrikaans settlement in the western Kalahari represents a white group who have been neither a colonial nor an economic power. Politically, socially and economically unimportant, they have also been isolated from fellow Afrikaners and the events which have given Afrikanerdom much of its distinctive cast.

These people now find themselves part of an independent yet democratic state, in which the numerically preponderant Tswana naturally hold nearly all high political office, and dominate the civil service. It is a state committed to non-racialism. Economically still very dependent on racially structured South Africa, it nevertheless constantly affirms its ideological independence by this policy. In so doing it finds itself marginally out of step with independent states to the north whose Africanisation programmes give preferential consideration to indigenous black inhabitants.[9] The parallel Botswana programme is one of localisation, the replacement of expatriates by citizens, irrespective of race.

The Ghanzi situation gains piquancy from the fact that Afrikaners have a reputation for racialism second to none, and although the impetus for this reputation derives from contemporary political practice in South

Africa, most textbooks stress that it has been an integral aspect of Afrikanerdom from the very early days of Dutch settlement at the Cape.

In selecting the Afrikaners of Ghanzi we were selecting what we took to be a traditionally race-conscious and reputedly racialist group who had, under seventy years of British rule, achieved some kind of *modus vivendi* with other ethnic groups in the vicinity, and who had with Independence become incorporated into a non-racial black state. We were interested in the history of their settlement as it demonstrated the relationships established between them and the British authorities; between them and the hunting and gathering Bushmen; between them and the Kgalagari who have been widely dispersed in the Kalahari for some centuries; between them and the powerful Batawana to the north, sometime overlords of the Ghanzi veld, from whom the concession to settle whites had been wrested by Rhodes in the late nineteenth century (Tlou 1972); between them and members of various other ethnic groups, Herero, Tswana and Coloured who came to farm, to work, and, more recently, to administer the district.

In the three months before we left England for the Kalahari, as we planned the project, the myths about Ghanzi Afrikaners began to accumulate.

> Don't forget to go into their family system. They are all in-bred; you'll find incest, the lot.

> Their cattle are so wild that they have to hunt them with guns.

> One of them didn't like the dances at the hotel so he shot the piano to bits.

> One of them took off all his clothes to run naked up a sand dune at midnight.

A local expatriate official to whom we wrote for advice was explicitly discouraging. 'Think again . . . I've been here for two years and I've not yet even found all their houses.'

Their houses are indeed widely dispersed, often thirty kilometres apart, reached by a network of sandy truck ruts in which the inexperienced driver is certain to get incessantly bogged down until he learns to drive with half inflated tyres and an essential resignation to delays. But the people were mundane enough when we eventually reached their simply furnished self-built houses. They responded with initial caution to our interest in them, their life style, and their world view, but they warmed to our central research technique, the recording of their oral history. Over the six-month fieldwork period they extended to us a tolerant hospitality which exceeded our expectations.

8

In telling us their history they told us who they were, who their ancestors had been, and how and why they lived in relative isolation from the technological devices and comforts which most whites take for granted. But they told us more. Perhaps unwittingly they told us about how they saw the other people round about and the kinds of relationships they had established with them. They talked about the independence of Botswana and contrasted the political turmoil of the rest of southern Africa with the orderly transfer of power in Botswana.

We remained outsiders. If what we received from these people was an edited version of their world view then we must credit them with a sophistication and flexibility which augurs well for their adaptation in the future. But first we look to their past.

2

Boers, trekboers and *bywoners*: 1898–1930

I

The early history of the Ghanzi region of the Kalahari is not clearly known, but it seems that until comparatively recently it was the almost exclusive territory of hunting and gathering Bushmen as it had been for 20 000 years. The steady southward movement of the Bantu had taken place beyond the periphery of the desert and it was not until the nineteenth century that population expansion, political change and the immense movements of peoples then taking place in southern Africa began to bring significant and increasing change into the Kalahari itself.[1]

The Kwebe–Gobabis limestone ridge rises slightly out of the endless sandveld of the Kalahari, a great shallow depression across the centre of southern Africa. Here alone on the ridge the spasmodic desert rains are cupped in rock and replenished by springs in the limestone. A good rainfall can maintain springs here for as long as seven years. There are seasons in the sandveld after rain when the pans fill with water and the Kalahari vegetation burgeons with a vivid greenness, but such seasons are rare and brief and water quickly evaporates. In the past the more reliable water supply at Ghanzi brought immense quantities of game there, both large and small. Passarge in 1907 considered that it was at Ghanzi alone that a reliable food supply had enabled Bushmen to establish a more elaborate economic and political structure than elsewhere (1907:114–24). The climatic and ecological advantages explain both the Batawana claim to suzerainty over the Ghanzi veld as far south as Okwa and as far east as Rietfontein, and the selection of this area as a centre for settlement by whites.

The first white man to settle on the Ghanzi ridge was Hendrik van Zyl. Little is known about him but extravagant myths are still told in Ghanzi of his double-storeyed house at Ghanzi Pan in the 1870s, filled with French period furniture and a hundred Bushman concubines, and of his great

10

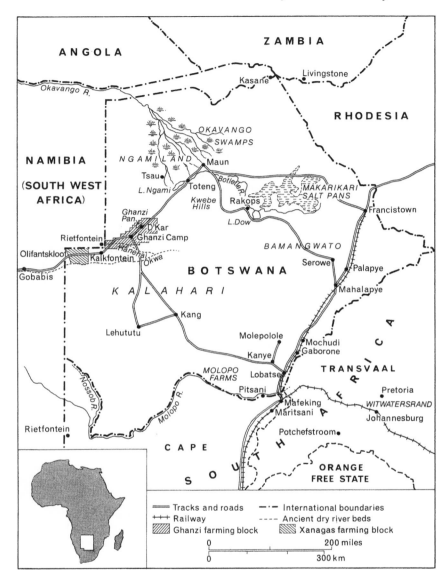

Fig. 4. Botswana and adjacent territories

dealings in ivory. More firmly established historically are his relations
with the Tawana. In 1879 he led a deputation for Moremi II, the Tawana
chief at Lake Ngami, to Coates Palgrave, who noted the very large grant
of land he enjoyed from Moremi, as well as the presence of trekboers

11

'north west of the Lake' with whom van Zyl was 'on friendly terms'.[2] Van Zyl's subsequent violent death may have been as much to do with a change in Tawana leadership as to any serious dispute between himself and the Tawana.

In the early nineteenth century a party of trekkers struggling on foot after being forced to abandon their wagons in the central Kalahari had reached Ghanzi 'in a despairing state' (Andersson 1857:368). The trekboers who passed by Ghanzi Pan in the 1870s were later to remember it as a unique place of fountains and open waters, and Lake Ngami to the north as limitless water fed by the seasonal flooding of the Okavango. This was also the impression of the traveller Baines who wrote of the water in Ghanzi Pan as 'so large that a man lying in wait for game at one end was often disappointed of a shot by the animals drinking at the other' (Baines 1864:146). A few years earlier Andersson had called it 'a peculiar and dreary looking place consisting of an extensive hollow with innumerable small stones scattered over its surface . . . hemmed in with thorn coppices' (Andersson 1857:369). In the 1890s the Barolong had appeared along the dry Okwa riverbed, moving westwards to escape the new burden of taxation in the east of the Protectorate.[3] By this time the gun trade through Ghanzi had become so considerable as to merit a proposal from the Resident Magistrate in Ngamiland that a colonial outstation be established on the Okwa to halt gun-running on the 'Damara Road', as the ancient waterless riverbed came to be known.[4]

The 1898 settlement of whites at Ghanzi was intended to be more permanent and a more organised event than any of these. In 1894 Izaak Bosman, agent of the British South Africa Company, announced by distributed pamphlets and newspaper advertisements in the *Zuid Afrikaan* and *Die Patriot* the availability of blocks of land for settlement 'in the vicinity of Lake Ngami . . . twelve thousand morgen blocks for settlement on the highveld [the Kwebe–Gobabis ridge] and three thousand morgen on the low-veld . . . beside the Lake, for agricultural purposes'.[5]

Various explanations have been advanced to account for the 1898 trek to Ghanzi. The activities of Bosman and the links between him, the British South Africa Company and the colonial administration have no doubt helped to promote the idea that the Ghanzi settlement was simply a device for halting possible German expansion from the west. So long as the Bosman Concession included claims to both Ngamiland and Ghanzi, such a buffer strip might arguably have had some purpose, but once recognition of the Ngamiland Concession was refused, the relatively minor settlement of fifty scattered and poor families cannot have been anticipated to present any decisive obstacle to German imperial ambitions. The delay between the official initial reconnaissance under Fuller in 1895 and the formal settlement in 1898 suggests in any case that strategic considerations were far from paramount. It is likely that, perceiving that the restless trekking of the Afrikaners could not be halted, Rhodes resolved to ensure that trekker movement, and possible trekker settlement, would be used to secure the Company's claims rather than potential boer republican territorial ones.[6] In the Cape Assembly in 1894 he had said, 'As to the advisability of the trek, the people could not be stopped from trekking; they would not remain in the country; they might just as well try to stop a river.'[7]

When High Commissioner Milner met Rhodes in Umtali in 1897 he agreed that the number of trekkers at Ghanzi would be kept as near to fifty families as possible, and would in no case exceed sixty. He further agreed that the Ghanzi settlement should not be seen as establishing 'a right of occupation of vacant land in the Protectorate by any other party except with the concurrence of the Company',[8] and this despite the fact that the transfer of the administration of the Protectorate to the Company had just been postponed *sine die*. It would be hard to find a more eloquent expression of the delicate balance that Rhodes and Milner sought at that time between conflicting forces.

The trekkers who were recruited for the Ghanzi settlement were a little surprised that the trekking upon which they had for so long been engaged should suddenly become cause for payment and aid from the British South Africa Company, but they gladly accepted the subsidy which Rhodes offered.[9] Some of them joined the exploratory trek of officials and Bechuanaland Border Police, under Fuller, which crossed the Kalahari from Molepolole to Ghanzi in seventy-nine days in 1895.[10] Fuller's mission was to determine the border with the Batawana and also to mark out farms. At Kgoutsa on the Ghanzi ridge Fuller established a defensive laager; fearing both Bushmen and Batawana he allowed only half the party to be away at any time, exploring the environment. Those prospective settlers who were present chose farms, drew lots to settle disagreements, and were issued with certificates of ownership endorsed by Mr McDermid and the Rev. Adriaan Hofmeyr representing the British South Africa Company. The trek then returned to Pitsani where their relations were waiting.

On 28 October 1897 Milner personally met the 'Ngami trekkers' who came to the Maritsani railway siding at 6 p.m. as his train came through. His Excellency assured them, 'Mr Hofmeyr interpreting', that 'Segkome was prepared to renounce all rights' to 'this Ghanzi country' which was now 'part of the Queen's Dominions', provided that 'the country actually occupied by him in the vicinity of Lake N'Gami is guaranteed to him'. He assured them that 'Her Majesty's Government is willing . . . to deal with the Ghanzi District as vacant land, over which Segkome will have no right

13

whatsoever. It is also willing to settle upon you this vacant land.' Should the administration of the country at some future time pass into the hands of the Chartered Company this would make no difference to them.[11]

It was not until July 1898 that the trekkers finally departed for Ghanzi. Unlike Fuller's trek they took the so-called river road, skirting the worst thirsts by travelling along the north-eastern fringe of the desert through Serowe, Tsienjane and along the winding course of the Botletle towards Kwebe. They used the traditional wagon pulled by an ox team. Capacious, sturdy, riding on iron-rimmed hardwood wheels, the wagons were covered with a sail over a bent wood frame. Tools, provisions and a few possessions were carried in the long stinkwood or *hardekool* chests that were lashed in place on either side of the wagon. Unlike American 'wagon trains' entering hostile country, the trekkers spread out as they travelled slowly northward with their few cattle, a day's ride or more apart.

It was a hard trek in 1898. The land was exceptionally dry during the winter and the cattle suffered severely. Afterwards people spoke of the 'terrible heaviness of the river road and the parched up state of the country'.[12] Those acquainted with the direct route to the Ghanzi veld, from Molepolole due west, said that they much preferred that route, 'for although the thirsts were individually longer they are no worse in aggregate and food can be obtained en route while the cattle seem to suffer less'. The river road had the additional and important disadvantage of almost doubling the distance to be covered. Though Drotsky and van der Linde, the first two trekkers to arrive, made the journey to Ghanzi in three months, the last of the party arrived after seven months on the river road.

By the end of October 1898 eleven families had arrived in Ghanzi and had been allotted farms by Major Panzera, Special Commissioner for Ngamiland, who had been made responsible for finally apportioning land and surveying and mapping the land grants. One of those families had lost three oxen and two horses en route, and had been forced to cut their wagon in half, converting it into a light Scotch cart, in order to complete their journey. It was February 1899 before the last of the original trekking party arrived.

Altogether forty-one farms were allocated, a figure which included farms for those still struggling to complete the trek. Significantly the farms along the northern (Batawana) border were allocated to what Panzera described as 'reliable colonial or English people'. The farms were laid out about available open waters in the pans scattered through the district. In order to share the available water equitably members of the same family were allotted farms around one pan. Quit rent on each farm was fixed at the sum of £5 per annum.[13] Each farm was approximately 5000 morgen (6.5 kilometres squared), except in the case of Drotsky who, in recognition of his services to the trek and his assistance to Panzera, was given a grant of 6000 morgen which, Drotsky argued, would allow for an equal division of his land into three 2000 morgen farms for his three sons.

From the beginning of the settlement there existed considerable confusion in the colonial mind about the trekkers. Little is known or remembered of the first years. Panzera, before leaving Ghanzi, wrote glowingly of the garden Drotsky had laid out,[14] but in 1902 only one trekker family, the Talyaards at D'Kar, thirty kilometres north-east of Ghanzi, remained. Gillett's comment (1969) on that situation, that the trekkers intended to abandon Ghanzi altogether, reflects the same category of misunderstanding that prompted Milner, in 1904, to write that 'the settlement of European farmers at Ghanzi has not proved a success'.[15]

Terms like 'settlement', 'European' and 'farmer' easily obscure the fact that the people so described were neither settled, European, nor farmers, but trekkers, a fact which alone explains much of the failed expectations on both sides, and the marked hostility which characterised colonial attitudes to trekkers in the western Kalahari. Ghanzi in 1898 was a wilderness, and it would be difficult to conceive how a settlement of European farmers there could ever have been successful. The High Commissioner himself clearly had his doubts, for at his meeting with the trekkers at Maritsani in 1897 he had specifically warned them to 'consider well before you start whether you have evidence enough that the land will support you. . . . It is right that I should tell you that persons who have lately come from there say that it is different from what it was . . . that there is not sufficient pasturage, that there have been two years of terrible drought and that an adequate water supply cannot be counted upon.'[16]

II

Isolated by great expanses of waterless dry land which was penetrable with safety only after a season of heavy rain, the Ghanzi trekkers occupied virgin Kalahari veld. It seems unlikely that they ever considered that they were or should be 'European farmers'. Nothing would have been more inappropriate to the vagaries of the Ghanzi environment than to settle and farm.

Existence at Ghanzi, even in the deceptively green seasons of rain and abundance, was always tenuous. A delay or decline in rainfall, a prolongation of the summer heat, could easily cause open waters to disappear. Game migrated swiftly with changes of grazing, and cattle were constantly exposed to the risk of drought. The trekker economy, rather than being oriented to distant centres of white settlement, was local: an amalgam of hunting, gathering, transhumance, erratic subsistence agriculture and exchange trading. There was little option open to them but isolation from white settler society, and this may have been exactly their intention.

Rhodes and Milner had sought to establish firm limits on the numbers allowed to settle, but the difficulties of maintaining close control over migration, and the end of the Chartered Company's liability for subsidising settlement, caused these limitations to lose their urgency. From 1902 a small but steady movement of trekkers into Ghanzi continued. Some remained but a short time before moving on. Others stayed longer. Many paid no quit rent; they were *bywoners* (literally 'those who live with') but the distinction was purely legalistic. Those who paid rent were usually as poor as those who did not.

The restlessness of the trekkers, their constant need to hunt, to move into new places, to go trading for cattle amongst surrounding people, and to search for game trophies, particularly ivory, contribute to a picture of much coming and going for the next forty years. The close ties between the earlier Angola trekkers and Ghanzi were retained. Some people moved northwards into Angola almost immediately after the 1898 settlement, and many moved back to Ghanzi and neighbouring Gobabis in Namibia when disillusionment with the Portuguese led to repatriation and migration in 1928. There were also ties between the Afrikaners of the western Kalahari and those settled in Molepolole by the Bakwena after they failed in an attempt to cross the Kalahari in 1894 (Malherbe 1939).

In 1910 Izaak Bosman, in association with one of the original Ghanzi trekkers, attempted to organise meetings throughout the Transvaal and the Cape, to advertise the farming and settlement possibilities of Ghanzi, to mobilise pressure upon the government to sanction further white settlement, and to found a settler organisation. In 1910, 1913 and 1914 there were abortive attempts to organise treks from Upington, Gordonia and Narogas, where there appears to have been heavy pressure on available land and an awareness of the sparsely populated reaches of the Ghanzi veld.[17] At a meeting in Upington in 1914, 300 families who had been 'ousted' by 'speculators, Jews and others' planned to depart for Ghanzi, encouraged in their choice by rumours of 350 Dutch trekkers who had preceded them.[18] None of these attempts succeeded, though it seems likely that many of the families who subsequently trekked to Ghanzi, including Kotze, the Christian blacksmith who was to found the *dopper* congregation there, came because of the interest stimulated by these attempts.

Most of the trekkers who came in 1898, and many of those who came later, had trekked before. They did not come raw from a settled rural life to plunge into the capricious Kalahari existence. Their trekker skills of generations were based on Nama and Bushman knowledge of veld foods. They knew how to live frugally on gathered green vegetables, berries, fruits and roots, and how to make a coffee substitute from the seeds of the *koffiepeel* bush or the dried roots of the *witgat* tree. They knew that *tsamma* melons provide water for man and beast through the long thirsts. They relied on meat from the hunt, which they ate fresh or preserved dried as *biltong* or in highly spiced sausage.

They could cure skins and tan leather for clothes and furnishings; steenbok for soft yellowish jackets, hartebeest for tough leather trousers. 'But the people did not wear them much, only if they could not afford the other, you know. The leather gets very hot for this climate.' They made their own shoes. Special care was exercised in the preparation of the thick heavy shoulder hide of rhinoceros and wildebeest for tough *riems* for harnesses and tethers. All possessed this kind of knowledge but some had additional skills in the making and repairing of wagons and furniture. Almost all men had some knowledge of metals but only a few were true smiths, shaping the great wagon springs, rimming and binding the wheels, fashioning tools and implements. Ultimately what was to be the most decisive trekker skill was the digging and construction of wells. Techniques for shoring up excavations and knowledge of dynamite enabled the trekkers to dig lower levels for water than would otherwise have been possible.

They came with small herds of goats, occasional sheep, and cattle. Like their black neighbours they regarded cattle as social wealth, not in the narrow pecuniary sense of a commercial economy but as the proper social foundation underpinning family and community life. Cattle were seldom slaughtered, except on occasions of rare importance. Goat was preferred as meat. Each child was given a beast at birth to provide, through successive progeny, the nucleus of a small herd, as in the Tswana *tshwaiso* system. The practice of poorer men herding wealthier men's cattle in return for milk and a share of the offspring was, in its generosity, closer to the Nama than the Tswana institution of *mahfisa* (Schapera 1930, 1938). An extensive specialised vocabulary described the varieties of cattle, their colour, markings, posture, horn formation and age. It persists today, witness to the intense preoccupation with cattle, and their importance in social life. In 1973 thirty-six Afrikaans phrases to describe cattle were recorded, excluding breed names.

Few trekkers, either renters or *bywoners*, chose to build themselves permanent houses. In 1922 there were only thirteen houses in the Ghanzi area according to Stigand's careful map, yet in 1920 sixty-three of the 'farmers and residents' of the area had signed their names on a petition to the High Commissioner.[19] Two or three of the thirteen houses were built of roughly dressed limestone, plastered internally, with unglazed shuttered windows, single-storeyed under a thatched roof. One of these at D'Kar was visited in 1928 by the Imperial Secretary who, at the invitation

17

of the High Commissioner, had organised an expedition 'from Maha-lapye westward across the unknown Kalahari direct to Ghanzi'. He

> called at a farm owned by a man named Talyaard. He spoke English quite well, and provided us with fresh milk, butter, bread and eggs. His wife wore a variety of white starched linen bonnet, and her features and dress were so characteristically Dutch that she might have stepped straight from a Flemish canvas. The manner in which they had maintained European standards in this lonely place, hun-dreds of miles from the nearest centre of civilisation, excited my unstinted admiration.

> (Clifford 1930:354)

The other houses were substantial wattle and daub dwellings of an indigenous African style, with a thick overhanging thatch to provide a shady *stoep* (verandah) on three sides. The floors were repaired weekly with fresh applications of dung and water. Others lived more simply, using a wagon or Scotch cart as the focus about which their encampment was made. Some built smaller wattle houses with dung and mud walls, 'like the kaffirs'. None in the generous Kalahari sun needed particular shelter except against seasonal rain. The cold desert nights could be warded off wrapped in a Nama fur blanket, or *kaross*, before a fire. Such small temporary houses, which were still in use in the 1960s, were doubtless too insignificant for inclusion on Stigand's maps, or for mention in the acting Resident Magistrate's report of 1920. In overlooking them the administrators were upholding the accepted colonial distinction be-tween houses (European) and dwellings (indigenous).[20]

These early trekkers were almost self-sufficient, but their appetite for stock, like that of most pastoralists, was not easily satisfied. Ghanzi was good cattle country, but it was also good lion country, and the absence of any fencing or control over cattle during calving meant that predators, as well as drought and sickness, could entirely destroy any hope of natural increase in the herd. Thus the trekkers sought to maintain and supple-ment their herds with traded stock. They also wanted cereals, especially maize for grinding into the staple *mieliemeel*. Maize could be grown in Ghanzi but owing to drought and infestation the crop was never reliable and seldom adequate, though the petitioners in 1920 were probably exaggerating when they claimed 'every six years, we can only reckon on a crop once in that time'.[21]

The Barolong along the Okwa, the Kgalagari and later the Herero sometimes traded stock with the trekkers, but the volume of such trade was limited. Only on the better watered, more fertile soil of Ngamiland was a surplus of grain available. Furthermore, the Batawana had an appe-tite for the goods and services that trekkers could provide. The Batawana

Fig. 5. Afrikaner and his wife at home on the *stoep*

perceived the advantages of having wood and iron workers close at hand, experienced in constructing carts and wagons capable of replacing the traditional Batawana sledge. They were willing to barter for trekker manufactures, but above all they valued trekker ability to sink deep wells, and for this they were prepared to trade cattle and maize.

The Batawana wells were sited in the beds of seasonal rivers or pans. Their location in the dangerously soft soil meant that they were seldom more than pits, threatened by the lowering of the water table which has continued until the present.

> Our people could dig better wells than the *outas* there [recalled an old Afrikaans woman]. In Sehitwa you had to dig wells in sand and the ones they dug used to fall in. The wells had to be propped with tar props from the bottom to the top. Our men used to dig wells with a spade and then use a winder to turn the sand out; and then when they reached the stone, they blasted it out with dynamite. Some wells were a hundred feet deep. People worked at the bottom of the well and two or three stayed above to get rid of the sand. My father was a specialist in well digging.

This early trade was a matter of direct initiative and face to face contact. In this, as in many other respects, the Afrikaners conformed to social patterns established long before their arrival. 'We bought cattle from the Kaffirs. We made *veldskoene* [shoes] and exchanged from for

19

cattle. We also did blacksmith's work for them when they got wagons. We made wagons for them and so the one worked for the other. They were never *snaaks* [literally "funny, peculiar", perhaps "unpredictable"].'

The economic relations of the Afrikaners with their neighbours to the north thus provided a framework of pragmatic interdependence, though the Batawana, longer established on their more fertile soil, held the upper hand. In 1919 in a time of grain shortage Chief Mathiba's suspension of grain exports to Ghanzi evinced great Afrikaner concern. The Batawana for their part valued the Ghanzi community as a source of cattle exchanges, though Pim in 1933 estimated this trade to be in steady decline – 'it probably does not amount to over 2000 [cattle] per annum'. During the periodic closures of the Batawana's northern trade route to the mines of the Congo, northern Rhodesia and Angola, trade to the south became even more important, not only with Ghanzi, but through Ghanzi, into and through the Kalahari to Johannesburg (Pim 1933:127).

There were normal mutual animosities and tensions over grazing, cattle and territory, which were occasionally expressed in ponderous petitions to a distant government. 'We object to thousands of cattle being driven over our farms, trampling all our grasses and underbred Kaffir bulls mixing with our breeding stock. We never receive no benefit whatsoever therefrom';[22] but these disgruntlements were contained within this framework.

III

In the early years Afrikaners felt little need to engage actively in commercial cattle trade, except in exchange for the few commodities which were not locally obtainable: sugar, tea, coffee, cloth and ammunition. These were available from the occasional *smous* (itinerant hawker) or from the trading store at Tsau in Ngamiland, some three hundred kilometres to the north. The trading stores would pay partly in cash, partly in a credit note or 'goodfor', the balance between parts being determined by the trader's need to dispose of his purchases (Pim 1933:128). Whereas credit notes involved a bookkeeping transaction, 'goodfors', 'the note the native gets compelling him to come back to the same store to make his purchases', often changed hands and became a semi-negotiable currency.

The traders were drawn to Ngamiland by its cattle wealth and the numerous population the region was able to support. In 1921 the Batawana Reserve, with 17 500 people and 104 000 cattle, was the second most populous district in the Protectorate; only Bamangwato had more people and cattle. The whole Ghanzi District by contrast had a population of only 1700, of whom 142 were whites. Their isolation severely limited the options open to them. In 1913 an official observer had reported that 'the farmers are almost entirely in the hands of the traders and are practically obliged to accept whatever the trader likes to offer them for their cattle'.[23] Some attempted to bypass traders by taking cattle out to the market directly, but this was feasible only with a fairly large herd which required cooperation and organisation, or wealth.

As early as 1913 two men of substance had emerged in Ghanzi, Lewis and Hardbattle, to be followed later by Burton, each owning five to six hundred head of cattle as against an average holding of a few head, which might rise in good times to thirty or forty. The predominance of non-Afrikaner names among these early successful entrepreneurs is undoubtedly significant. It is also somewhat misleading. There had been four English-speaking families amongst the original forty-one trekkers, and there were as many as eighteen in Ghanzi in 1938. After the original settlement, as the reality of Kalahari 'farming' became obvious, English numbers steadily declined and the Afrikaner proportion increased. The few determined and successful English-speaking farmers succeeded in part by extensive local adaptation. Burton, a New Zealander, became head of an Afrikaans family by marriage. Hardbattle, one time Bechuanaland policeman, took as common law wife the child of a white settler by a Bushman woman. Lewis, despite his name, was an Afrikaner. The name has been Afrikanerised for several generations and is pronounced 'Le Vees'. Members of the family retain the recollection that their ancestor came from 'Vahliss' (Wales) near England.

The accumulation of relatively large herds did not bring about change in the life style of their owners, but was of importance to the rest of the community, since the tradition was to lend cattle out to the poorer members of the community, especially to *bywoners*. This practice not only created an opportunity for the poor to acquire wealth in a world of cattle, but, by mobilising a conscientious herding work force, was probably alone in making possible the establishment of relatively large herds in the vastness of unfenced Ghanzi veld.

Early Afrikaner concern over trek routes out of Ghanzi reflected their limited trade ambitions. In 1909 they suggested that a new trek route be established from Ghanzi to Molepolole which would 'not only open up the Kalahari country but will also shorten the distance to Ngamiland by at least 200 miles'.[24] There were great risks attending the trekking of cattle through the long thirsts via Lehututu, the customary route which could 'only be used with any degree of safety in years when there has been a good rainfall'.[25] It was three nights trekking to Okwa, where the first water after Ghanzi was available, and a further two hundred kilometres of thirst lay between Okwa and the water of Lehututu. 'If you understand driving cattle well, then you let them walk at ease at their own pace, you don't hurry them. You let them walk just as you let them walk on the farm. Then they arrive in good condition. It takes twenty-six days at an easy pace.'

As the one or two members of the Ghanzi community began to establish large herds, the previously spasmodic trade in cattle began to develop as a specialised but hazardous entrepreneurial activity. A few men, professional cattle trekkers rather than pastoralist farmers, entered the trade, exchanging immature or poorly nourished beasts from Ngamiland for fattened stock in Ghanzi under the 'two for one' system. Mounted on donkeys ('the donkeys were much stronger than horses who take fright and too easily run amok'), they would move through the Kalahari, at night, balancing the risks of cattle running wild at the sight of lions against the greater risks of dehydration due to excessive exertion in the heat of the day.[26] Once in the eastern Protectorate they would sell them to fattening ranches at Lobatse, or put them through quarantine onto the Johannesburg market. A few local men took part in this trade, earning a commission of five shillings per head ('But from that you had to pay the *volk* [the Bushman drovers]'). For most the costs in terms of months away from family and cattle were too great, and most of the trade was handled by outside entrepreneurs who even if they owned land at Ghanzi were seldom to be found there. Their primary interest often lay in the fattening ranches in the east.[27]

The establishment of a magistracy in Ghanzi in 1922 gave the first stimulus to the growth of regular transport riding. Government required not only supplies and food for the administration and its officers, but communications, and, with the advent of law and order, supplies to feed its prisoners.

Horses were still extremely rare. Oxen were widely used, not only under the *hardekool* ox yoke, but for riding, Nama style, guided by a ring in the nose (Wilson and Thompson 1969:62). 'The skin is very loose but when you learn to sit on it, you ride nicely, you don't get tired.' Donkey teams were favoured for transporting. The first postal contract for carrying mail from Gobabis to Ghanzi used donkeys. Hottentots carried the mail from Gobabis to Olifantskloof from where an Afrikaner and a Bushman carried it on to Ghanzi. The entire journey took about a month. They transported supplies as well as mail and the contractor remembers 'a nice deserted German house at Sandfontien where there was still a spring in 1928' where they would halt and rest for a few days. In other parts of the Protectorate letters were carried by 'native runner', sometimes for distances over 480 kilometres (Pim 1933:13).

The world depression of 1930 scarcely penetrated Ghanzi, disengaged as most settlers were from the economy of the wider Western world. But by coincidence a series of local disasters created a severe parallel local depression. In 1933 the district fell into the grip of a severe drought. To

Fig. 6. Father and son on trek with cattle through the Kalahari keep a constant watch for predators. (Reproduced by permission of Argus Africa News Service, Cape Town)

the north it was so bad that the Hambukushu took to the Okavango swamps in search of water.[28] In Ghanzi the Afrikaners began to lose cattle as open waters dried up. In 1934 wells also began to run dry. A simultaneous outbreak of foot and mouth disease in the east reached westwards to Rakops in 1934, involving a total embargo on all cattle movements, hitting entrepreneur, pastoralist and *bywoner* alike. Then the rains broke so torrentially that there was extensive flooding which attracted the anopheles southwards from the swamps. The malarial outbreak was officially reckoned at 100 per cent rate of infection on the Ghanzi farms, the Camp, Olifantskloof and Kalkfontein. A doctor and a dispenser were despatched from Mafeking with supplies of quinine.

Malaria might reasonably have been regarded as the final misfortune, but while the fever was still taking its toll the locust came stripping the veld and ensuring that the sparse crops that had been sown were devastated. Only two farmers reaped anything at all. In this final disaster Afrikaners were 'barely able to keep body and soul together'.[29]

Relief supplies were moved in from Gobabis, by lorry to the border and thence, as a policy of spreading the earnings of contract labour, by donkey wagon train to Ghanzi. Rations were distributed to all, but able-bodied men were expected to labour in return at roadmaking: whites on the route to Toteng in Ngamiland for one shilling and sixpence a day, blacks on the Ghanzi to Gobabis road with no cash payment.

> My father worked for one and six a day, and my husband too, before we got married. And they got *mieliemeel* and a little tea or coffee, rations, because we had no food. The men worked on the roads, cutting the new roads. They lived on the roads and came home at weekends. We used to ride ten miles to school on donkeys when my father worked the roads.

Extract from transcript of tape recording, Ghanzi, 1973

Speaker: White Afrikaans woman, aged 57
  Occupation: Hawker
  Divorced, adult children
  Place of birth: Angola
  Citizenship: South West Africa
  Land owned: nil
  Other property: two-roomed house

Our ancestors trekked from the Transvaal. My father was a boy when they trekked through Ghanzi, and from here to Rietfontein; there the people got sick and some of them died of fever. Then my father's family went on to Angola. He was sixteen at the time, he had been born in the Koakoaveld round about 1880.

24

I was born in 1916 at Humpata in Angola. Humpata is the town, the place where we actually stayed was Ooikihingi. There my mother died when her youngest child was eight hours old. I was then nine or ten.

In Angola we had cattle. Most people had cattle. It's a very fertile land with rivers. We did not have windpumps or engines, there were springs. My father used to go out with ox wagons and chop down trees, and cut them into nice rectangles and take them and sell them to the Portuguese as planks, and they gave us money. Then we used to buy salt and take it to the Ovambos and the Moemoeryas, and exchange for mealies. We went on ox wagons, three or four days' journey.

There were more than two hundred Afrikaans families there. We had farm schools and not many teachers. The teacher was the one who had more education than the rest. Children did not go to school every day. When I came to South West I could not read or write but I knew how to count. A *predikant* came two or three times a year to baptise the children.

When the Portuguese wanted us to give up our school and our church and our language we sent people to the Union [of South Africa] to ask, and they said we must come to South West. That was 1928. Not everybody left, some had married Portuguese and some trekked later. We left on ox wagons and went with the oxen as far as the Kunene river and we crossed the Kunene with the oxen. On the other side we got rid of the oxen and the wagons and the government transported us with lorries to Gobabis.

In South West I went to school and then I worked, any work. I cleaned houses and did washing and ironing in the houses of Afrikaners in Gobabis. I earned two pounds sixteen a month to wash the children's and teachers' clothes in the school. When I was bigger I went to work in Windhoek. I worked in a boarding house, then a hotel, six pounds ten shillings a month, that was 1940, with free board for myself and my two children.

I had a daughter with a club foot. They had given her an operation at Gobabis but they couldn't make the foot right. So I went to Cape Town to Groot Schuur hospital. I stayed there for eight months. I worked. First I worked for a doctor – a heart specialist – for three pounds a month, washing with a machine, ironing, cooking, polishing floors. In Rondebosch. It was too little for my children. So I got work in a shirt factory for one pound seven shillings a week. But I was happy the day they said you can take your child and go. I cried a lot and came straight away.

I stayed for a while on my father's farm, thirty or forty miles out of Gobabis. I made charcoal for people. I took my two children and an axe and a spade and I went out. You make a big fire but as they burn out you must put them out with water and sand, the easiest is sand. Then you put the charcoal in sacks.

After that I went to work at the school hostel. They came to look for me, to cook, six pounds and ten shillings a month. Then I married and in 1945 we came to Ghanzi.

We used to ride transport, my husband and I. We each had a licence. I got my heavy duty licence in 1947. We used to ride from Gobabis to Ghanzi and then to Maun. We also rode through the Kalahari to Lobatse. We carried mostly salt, sugar, petrol, diesel and beer, because there wasn't a hotel at that time.

Mr Midgely [pronounced 'Meatzlee'] was the Magistrate here. He said to me one day, 'Mrs Potgieter, you can get a café licence if you want to.' I said, 'What would it cost?' and he said, 'Ten pounds.' I had ten pounds saved so I took the money and bought the licence, and I went and rode to old Blake and asked him to lend me 150 pounds to begin with the café and he lent it to me. I started the café in the pantry in the big house at D'Kar. The *volk* [people, blacks] used to come a lot from Rhodesia and from Maun and they used to arrive in the night, wet and hungry. Then I used to get up. They used to come and knock and ask for food. I always baked bread and made them coffee and sold them bread and jam. Then I'd go back to sleep. Later I got a grocery licence, and a hawker's licence and a general dealer's licence. I built a little shop.

In 1957 my husband died and I was left. My husband had borrowed money before we were married, so the land wasn't mine to inherit. I rode transport by myself in a Chev lorry for the next four years until I remarried. Men were also riding lorries on that route. It was a pleasure to see how cross the men got if I took passengers away from them. We used to compete to see who could get the most passengers. Together with my new husband I rode transport for the government, petrol and that sort of thing, government contract. We also rode post before I handed the transport over to my son-in-law.

When my first husband died I had the option on his grazing land. I said I wanted it. I said, 'I'm not rich but I'll work and pay for it.' So I worked and saved and put by, and when I remarried we put down boreholes. When my husband and I were divorced I didn't see myself managing the farm alone with the Bushmen. It's a bit hard and so I decided to sell out and quit.

Now I am a hawker. I got my licence in 1956. I ride from place to place, I stop. The people come and buy. I ride a big lorry. I take material and tinned food and tea, tobacco and soap. I ride with five men [blacks]. I used to take a lot, now I think the fewer you take the better. They tramp on your things and break them. They're too lazy to load and unload properly. At nights we sleep out by the truck, the men on one side, and me on the other [she laughs].

I've got to go to Gobabis tomorrow to get my *mieliemeel* [maize meal] permit, then I'll bring in *mielies*, also tea and coffee. I enjoy living in the open and carrying on this business. It's my vocation. I don't know whether I'm going to be able to keep my hawker's licence. I have to ask for a residence permit. I'm a citizen of South West. In 1970 I asked for Botswana citizenship, but they said I must fill in the papers again.

26

3

Into the cash economy: 1930–72

I

In 1928 a trader with interests at Kalkfontein, 130 kilometres west of Ghanzi, brought the first lorry through Ghanzi. The lorry arrived in a roadless wilderness where deep shifting sand could seize a vehicle and hold it fast, finding its intrusive and destructive way into every part of the engine; where the jagged limestone of the ridge ripped tyres and snapped springs, and where seasonal rains could transform the desert tracks into a mire. In itself it seemed insignificant, but its arrival marked the beginning of the real involvement of Ghanzi in the modernising economy of cash. It cut the Ghanzi to Gobabis journey from four weeks to three days, and facilitated the more rapid flow of goods and services, slowly depriving the donkey teams of their labour-intensive purposes. It opened the distinction, at first slight, between those who had capital (usually cattle) to meet the demands of the changing situation, and those who did not. The quality of life began imperceptibly to change.

> We stayed well and friendly before the lorries came. Before the trucks came there was no money. Cattle went for two shillings. A fat cow was worth fifteen shillings. If you wanted to go to Gobabis it was with ox wagon. And the return journey could take months. But it was a freer life. You could hunt and shoot, you could do what you liked.

The transport trucks, each with their complement of Bushmen to dig and cut and lay branches to make passable tracks through deep sand, both initiated direct change in Ghanzi and slowly opened the eyes of the Ghanzi Afrikaners to the consumer horizons of an outside and foreign world. By 1938 several locally owned trucks were engaged on the run from Gobabis to Maun via Ghanzi. Gobabis was the rail terminal for goods and mail, and the latter item formed once again the contractual basis on which transport could easily be maintained. 'We had four-ton

27

lorries and there were no roads, we made our own. We took fuel and sugar and flour from South West to Maun for the Ngamiland Trading Company and to the Greeks, Bailey and Riley. We'd come back empty with empty drums, and sometimes passengers.' Occasionally they went on beyond Maun, north-eastwards to Livingstone or eastwards to Mahalapye. But most trade was with Gobabis, a link strengthened by innumerable family ties joining Ghanzi Afrikaners with Angola trekkers resettled in that region.

The absence of any satisfactory outlet for cattle delayed changes that might otherwise have come more quickly. The new abattoir in Lobatse, which might have further stimulated the trans-Kalahari cattle trekking trade, briefly opened in 1934, but closed in 1937 and remained shut until 1954. Treks continued on a small scale to the fattening ranches of the east. Not infrequently cattle were smuggled across the South African border. It was through smuggling that some of the successful entrepreneurs in 1973 were believed to have amassed their initial capital. It was ruefully remarked in the European Advisory Council in 1945 that half a million head of cattle had been smuggled over the South African border in defiance of the quarantine regulations and without any apparent ill effect on cattle in the Union.[1]

The difficulties of finding stock outlets and the growth of transport riding with lorries established a creaming trade. The practice presumably spread west to Ghanzi from the eastern Protectorate where 'the ready money nature of the trade appealed to the Native cattle owner ... balancing to some extent the loss in markets' (Pim 1933:131). Creaming was 'the old fashioned practice . . . of utilising surplus milk at the height of the lactation period for the manufacture of butter and cheese'. However, 'there is not much profit in the business to the dairy rancher and Native producer. At the best it is a poor return to both and were it not for the urgent necessity for ready money many would go out of business altogether and let the calves have the lot' (Pim 1933:132).

To the non-owner in Ghanzi who was herding borrowed cattle, creaming provided an opportunity to exploit the loan to the full, the major drawback being the labour cost: 'It's a big expense to cream; you have to keep a lot of *volk* to do the milking. We kept eight Bushmen to do the milking, but we don't anymore. When you give up creaming it means you can manage without the cream money.'

The cream, stored in water-cooled towers, was collected by truck and transported to Gobabis, initially for butter and cheese making, later to provide an essential element in early plastics manufacture. Creaming reached a peak in Ghanzi in the late 1950s,[2] providing an essential source of money for most Ghanzi Afrikaners and declining only with the new prosperity from the beef trade after Independence. By 1973 creaming was rare amongst Afrikaners, some of whom continued to transport cream for Kgalagari and Herero producers in the western Kalahari villages. But in 1939 no-one anticipated future prosperity. An official visiting Ghanzi in that year described how 'for most of them farming means to get hold of a few cattle and to hire a native to herd them. These are the sum total of their exertions' (Malherbe 1939). He also noted how few of them had taken up creaming.

The Second World War passed with little repercussion on the isolated Ghanzi community. *Ghanzi se wêreld* (the world of Ghanzi) remained a relatively self-contained universe. The cattle still roamed in great herds across the veld. 'It was a bloody hard job, riding forty miles or more to bring the cattle back. And the wildebeest came in by the thousand amongst them and were very troublesome, using all the grazing and then chasing the cattle and frightening them.'

People occasionally repaired the beacons which marked Panzera's grants of farms in 1898, but such demarcations were not important. 'There was no sense of property. If you found out about your cattle at another place you had to go and fetch them.' 'Everyone's cattle roamed freely, and calved unsupervised on the veld. The first man to get his brand on a calf, he owned it.'

In the dry winter months cattle became tractable, forced to come in to the kraals and to water near the wells and boreholes, but in the summer after rain when the pans filled they frequently became very wild and uncontrollable. In their grazing they followed the spasmodic and highly localised rainfall, an arrangement which preserved the more parched areas from over-grazing, but militated against creaming.

II

By 1947 Ghanzi had had its import quota of immature stock from Ngamiland fixed at one thousand head, while its exports to the east stood at between five and six thousand head annually, a take-off which was officially thought to be very low considering 'the wonderful possibilities of the healthy Ghanzi veld'.[3] The rumour of 'wonderful possibilities' was seized upon by the South African press, and 'widespread advertisement . . . persuaded people to trek to Ghanzi, to cheap if not actually free farms, labour and shooting, to new lands where they thought police, courts or payment of school fees could be ignored'.[4] Perhaps this was the last Afrikaner trek. In 1961 a sympathetic official was to look back on the 'new trekkers' as 'led into this Canaan by some rather improbable promises'.[5] By 1954 the new wave of white immigration from South Africa was sufficient to alarm both officials and older settlers, whose casual, intimate and informal patterns of economic and social organisation were suddenly confronted with the need to accommodate an influx of strangers, who, although Afrikaners, were neither kinsmen nor part of the Kalahari world. They created a disturbance disproportionate to their numbers: twenty-three immigrant families were listed by the District Commissioner in 1954. Owing no loyalty to the traditional community leaders, the newcomers were quick to exploit the tensions between themselves and the British officials, who described them alternatively as 'squatters on Crown land, sponging off Burton to stock their farms'[6] and 'people of enterprise coming in with new ideas', who were undermining the traditional leaders' authority with 'ignorant locals'.[7]

> I came in 1951. I'd been visiting my uncle here, on and off, since I was twenty. I worked around, building, up in Ngamiland. Then in 1953 the story went round that you could get farms, grazing, five pounds a year, if you had a minimum of fifty cattle. I got one. I left Ngamiland in 1956 with seventy-two cattle, and lived for the next six years in a six by ten foot iron room, with my wife and two children. When it rained there were showers inside; it was hell in summer. . . . I used to buy a bag of meal on credit and all of us, even the labourers, were eating from the same bag. There wasn't money in those days. When the Bushmen collected payment they'd just go to the kraal and take cattle. I had a truck but there was no money for petrol so I go back to horse and cart and use that. We never had a goat or a sheep for slaughter, just living on small game. Sometimes you go for two or three days without a meal, and then when you've got a piece of meat again you appreciate it, really. It was nice, it was something.

Some newcomers brought new deep-boring water technology, which began to make water, and hence settlement opportunities, more widely available. Many new boreholes were on unallocated Crown land where the borers hoped to establish rights by virtue of their investment and enterprise. In March 1956 the Development Secretary advised that the land tenure chaos at Ghanzi demanded 'that the whole situation be regularised and controlled at the earliest'.[8] In 1957 the government-appointed surveyor began his work of 'regularisation' – redrawing farm boundaries in accordance with rational rather than traditional criteria, preliminary to the re-allocation of farms in accordance with economic rather than, again, traditional criteria.

The new trekkers had been quick to join the newly established Ghanzi Farmers' and Cattle Owners' Association, formed in 1951. It was itself a symptom of the erosion of informal community organisation, replacing, subtly, the traditional leadership with committee structures in which officials had as much chance of being heard, if not more, since English was

Fig. 7. Counting young stock for the local sale. The homestead is in the background

the dominant medium of the Association. The Farmers' Association symbolised the change that was occurring. Its primary task was the organisation of quarterly local cattle sales, providing an opportunity for speculators from the east to buy cattle locally. It also acted as a pressure group for the facilities and opportunities that the growing commercial farming required. Although most of the Afrikaans farmers joined it, and remained members, it has always had an English-speaking chairman, and a secretary able to keep minutes in English.

The idiom of the 1950s was development. The Colonial Development Corporation had agreed in 1954 to finance a vast ranching settlement in Molopo in the east and a new experimental frozen beef industry based on the revived abattoir at Lobatse, a scheme which farmers viewed with such scepticism that they threatened to boycott it.[9] The Ghanzi District Commissioner zealously pursued Protectorate development policy. In December 1957 the grading of a new sand road from Ghanzi to Lobatse had been completed, highway for the fifty-nine trucks then registered in the district. 'It is now possible to get to Lobatse in a day', reported the District Commissioner,[10] not without some pride, since the endeavour had consumed the whole of his financial allocation for that year, and had been undertaken with a single blade grader borrowed from Maun, 240

31

kilometres distant, and drawn by a farmer's truck along a bearing from Kang to Ghanzi taken by the one pilot in the district.

A new government-subsidised boarding school for local white children had been opened in 1953, bringing to an end an era of hired tutors and makeshift temporary family schools. Adjoining the school was a farm stocked with cattle paid as school fees by parents, where the children were to be taught 'the scientific approach to animal husbandry' to wean them from the 'old-fashioned notions' of their parents.[11]

To the long-established residents the new situation was challenging and threatening. They responded with a defensive gesture in the form of a petition drawn up in 1953 by a Mafeking solicitor who had recently acquired a farm in the Ghanzi District. The petition was signed by thirty-three Ghanzi residents and asked for the 'gradual' removal from the Ghanzi District of 'all Africans, all Coloureds and the results of admixtures of races' leaving 'the rights of Bushmen . . . undisturbed in this district' which would 'in future be allowed to develop as a European area'.[12]

The close parallel between the sentiments expressed in the petition and the policies of apartheid which in South Africa were approaching their sixth year of triumphant and ruthless implementation, were apparent even to its designer, who in a covering letter stressed that the petition 'is in no way connected with the so-called Apartheid policy of the Union of South Africa'.[13] Rather the issue was development, and to lend credibility to the point the petition also requested

> that the influx of poor whites should be stopped completely . . .
> whom your petitioners believe cannot in the long run benefit the
> district but who will eventually become a serious problem which in
> other parts of Southern Africa has taken many years to eradicate
> . . . these persons, for economic reasons generally are not in a
> position to fence or provide adequate water points for their cattle
> nor to ensure that the district is kept free of stock diseases.

Nevertheless it was the proposed explicit exclusion of Africans which rankled. The administration responded to the petition with rigorous disapproval, ordering an immediate confidential enquiry into the economic and political standing of each of the signatories. Thoroughly alarmed, several petitioners withdrew their signatures, and at a well-attended meeting of the Farmers' Association in April 1954 a motion that the Association 'disassociate itself entirely from the petition' was carried by 'a show of hands'.[14]

The petition affair was puzzling. The District Commissioner was perplexed by the reference to poor whites 'particularly as . . . not a few of the residents who have signed the petition could themselves be classed as poor whites'.[15] The veterinary department was perplexed at the apparent wish to exclude the Kgalagari from the district since 'Burton and Lewis, the two instigators of the petition are today allowing the following African stock to squat or remain on their freehold of leased farms: Cattle 1872; small stock 3832; equines 395; poultry 217; dogs 84'.[16] Some of the local farmers were perplexed. Six of them claimed that 'they had the wrong impression, they had not fully understood'.[17] Another wrote

> I have attended every meeting that has been held in Ghanzi with one or two exceptions since 1912 and I have never heard anyone ask to have the African and Coloured people removed out of the Ghanzi district . . . I personally don't think they should be moved out after all these years as I have never heard any complaint about them living here.[18]

The District Commissioner put the petition down to 'certain subversive influences', noting that the signatures had been obtained by 'very dubious methods' including bribes,[19] and rumours of government-sponsored resettlement in Ghanzi of two hundred Coloured persons from Lobatse.[20]

A major source of confusion was undoubtedly the use of the phrase 'Ghanzi District'. The petitioners were not, as was thought, seeking the removal of Kgalagari from Kalkfontein and other settlements, but merely asking to preserve the status quo.[21] But the damage was done. Local black insecurity was aroused as undoubtedly were animosities. In December 1953 the people of Karakobis at the *kgota* (village council) expressed the view that there was no point in deepening their wells since they had heard they were to be moved.[22] At a rowdy meeting of the Ghanzi Farmers' Association in May 1955 one of the signatories of the infamous petition complained that he had been called 'shit' by a black policeman and that there was no justice any more.[23]

The petition had been phrased with a typical boer bluntness, and although it received British outrage and indignation, the local segregation it suggested was not very different from English policy. 'Free-minded as we may be, I think we want to dwell more or less apart.'[24] The Divisional Commissioner of the northern Protectorate addressed a private memorandum on the Ghanzi petition to Mafeking suggesting that they had 'been too ready to place a sinister interpretation on the document . . . the conception of European settled blocks is not new in Africa . . . the idea as often as not has the support of all races. . . . This arrangement makes for great harmony between the races.'[25] When the farms were offered for sale five years later, the government came very close to implementing the 1954 petition. Economic criteria dominated the selection of freeholders, but only whites were invited to apply; Coloured and 'admixtures of races' were segregated at Xanagas some 150 kilometres to the west. Long-established local residents were given preferential purchase terms over newcomers.

III

Farms were offered at a low price, one rand per morgen, and on easy terms: payable over fourteen years. But stringent conditions were attached to the sale. Each farm had to be ring-fenced on its perimeter. Drilled water had to be found yielding a minimum flow of 1200 gallons a day, and each farm had to be stocked with at least one bovine to each twenty-five morgen.[26] Some local applicants were refused farms because they were too poor; others, given farms, fell into arrears with the initial annual payment of about R250 (125) for 5000 morgen, and the farms were repossessed. The cruel coincidence of this new need for cash with a prolonged outbreak of foot and mouth disease prompted many people to leave Ghanzi. The most telling figures are probably those from the register of the *Gereformeerde* church at D'Kar which show a decline in membership from 168 in 1961 to 55 in 1966. The government moratorium on all outstanding payments on farms until January 1964 came too late for the poorer farmer, while those, unsuccessful in their initial bids for farms, who had been waiting around in hope of a reprieve, found themselves increasingly under pressure from newly property-conscious owners. Indeed *bywoning* had become illegal for hire purchasers, whatever their personal inclinations. The conditions of sale stipulated that only two adult male Europeans could reside on any one farm: in effect an insistence that farm labour be black.

To these economic pressures were added others of a very different kind as the British government awoke to the inevitability of independence for the Protectorate. In 1961 the new Legislative Council met for the first time. And although white members outnumbered black by two to one, and black attitudes were far from militant (Dr Molema speaking for the 'black section' spoke of the endeavour to make race relations 'sweet and durable and workable'), a change was afoot which the Afrikaner press in South Africa was ready to interpret with alarmist vigour, noting that 'the Bantu attitude to the farmers in the last few years has entirely changed' and predicting the closure of cattle markets attendant on 'political difficulties . . . threatening between South Africa and Botswana'.[27] Only a regional Dutch Reformed church newspaper viewed 'the possibility that natives will govern the Protectorate' with equanimity for the Afrikaner farmers.

> The Afrikaner is also a native of Africa, our home is here, our culture is deeply rooted in the bosom of this land, and if we want to,

we also get on best with the black people of this country. If we are really as we believe the cultural and intellectual superiors of the Bantu then you can behave yourself under a native government if you have enough tact and pluck.[28]

Other secular reports suggested a more systematic victimisation of Afrikaners. Through policies of anglicisation and eviction 'the Government of the Protectorate is busy putting the screws on them'.[29]

The most dramatic turning of the screw was the abrupt government decision on 22 November 1963 to integrate all schools in the Protectorate, including the Ghanzi school as from January 1964, though the publicity attending the subsequent Afrikaner boycott of the Ghanzi school probably lent the event a greater prominence than its practical significance warranted. The alternative practice of sending children to schools beyond the border was already well-established, as was dissatisfaction with the local school on the part of many families. At a public meeting to discuss the implications of the government decision an emotional consensus that school integration was unthinkable was reached. The decision was almost immediately regretted. 'Many of us have now realised how harmless non-racialism is. But we acted in haste and are repenting in leisure.'[30] By October 1966, when Independence was formally conferred, the Ghanzi farmers participated in the local celebration, contributing 'eight oxen and numerous goats' to the official *braaivleis* which was reckoned 'a great success'.[31]

Independence coincided with an upswing in world beef prices. Vacant farms, which in 1964 had seemed commercially so unattractive that despite wide advertisement in South Africa the government had been forced to drop the price by 25 per cent to be rid of them, were rapidly filled, but with a new kind of owner – the South African company, seeking cheap land and the high rewards of modern ranching. By example, but also by direct involvement as employed farm managers of the new company farms, the Afrikaners were drawn into profitable commercial cattle farming. Symptomatic of the new search for ready cash by the farmer with little capital is the recent increase in trucking cattle to the Lobatse abattoir. The biannual event of rounding up the herd and walking them six hundred kilometres to the market postpones for too long the realisation of profit. In an increasingly cash world, farmers are drawn into a continual weekly grind across the Kalahari, down on Mondays, back on Fridays, often carrying other men's cattle at sixteen rand per head in their hire-purchased trucks in an endeavour to keep abreast of their truck payments. The reward is a continual flow of cash, but the costs of trucking are high for those too poor to employ drivers. Many see it not as an innovation, but as a return to that lowly standby, ever resorted to by poor

Afrikaners when his rewards as a boer no longer seemed adequate, namely transport riding. Wives are particularly sceptical, as the following conversation nicely captures:

> *First wife:* Hendrik is going to ride transport.
> *Second wife:* Yena!
> *First wife:* He says it's just for his own cattle, to take them to the abattoir.
> *Second wife:* That's what they all say. Then they start taking other people's, to pay for the truck; then the truck breaks and they have to buy another one to pay for the repair of the first one, and so it goes.
> *First wife:* I said to Hendrik when I married him, Hendrik, I'll eat dry porridge with you every day, but the day you begin to ride transport I'm off.

The physical strains of trucking are considerable. Unlike cattle, trucks do not hold their value. Added to this is the constant anxiety that water pumps at home might fail, and go unreported by Bushman workers seized by nomadic whims, leaving the cattle waterless and dying. To the smaller farmer trucking is one of the major irrationalities of the new cash economy.

The value of land at Ghanzi has been transformed in a decade. In 1964 the government lowered the price of land sold by the state from one rand to seventy-five cents a morgen in an attempt to be rid of what it saw as an unattractive investment. In 1972 three farms thus acquired in 1965 for R13 987 were sold for R54 817. After improvements had been taken into account, the Ministry of Agriculture calculated that a profit of 160 per cent had been made. Furthermore the sales were to well-established white cattle speculators in the east, against whose high offer the 'smaller farmers' and 'local citizens from outside Ghanzi' could not compete. Despite this 'conflict' with their 'general policy' the Ministry felt power-less to intervene.[32]

Cattle sales from Ghanzi have climbed from a steady 5000 per annum in the 1940s and 1950s[33] to an impressive 17 810 in 1972.[34] Symbolising the change that is taking place is the enlarged list of Ghanzi farm names. Often devised at short notice under administrative pressure, they have a fairy-tale fantasy quality about them: Bunnyville, Snow White, Black Cat, Fairy Glen, Tally Ho! This alienated flippancy is a far cry from the earnest choice of an earlier generation (*Uitkoms*, Conclusion; *Vryheid*, Freedom; *Rusplaas*, Resting Place), who saw their farms as their place, to which they were uniquely attached, not merely one of a number of interchangeable tracts of land for the profitable fattening of cattle.

36

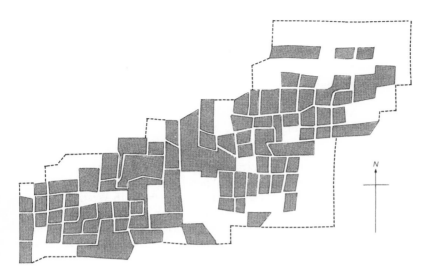

Fig. 8. Ghanzi farming block (1973 boundaries indicated by dotted line) showing distribution of land-holdings in 1960 after the granting of freehold. (Sources: List of demarcated farms in the Ghanzi District, 1938, BNA s 462/811; Applications from Ghanzi residents to purchase farms, 1959, BNA s 357/1; Farm names, Ghanzi District Development Officer's memorandum, 1973, mimeo)

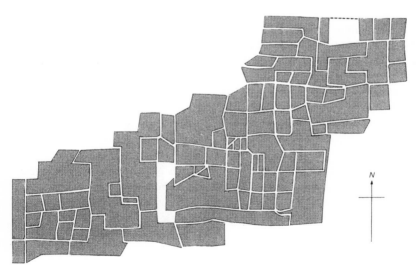

Fig. 9. Ghanzi farming block, 1973, showing expansion and consolidation of land-holdings. (Based on observations in 1973)

37

Into the cash economy

Extract from transcript of tape recording, Ghanzi, 1973

Speaker: White Afrikaans man, aged 55
 Occupation: farmer
 Married, adult children
 Place of birth: South West Africa
 Citizenship: Motswana
 Land owned: 12 000 morgen

I was a poor white when I came into this country in 1931. I had nothing, I had to make my life here. I was a transport rider. The first lorries to come here were those of me and my brother. When I first came there were no roads, just wagon trails. It took two full days to reach South West.

We made good money bringing petrol to the mine recruiting company in Maun, who recruited for the Witwatersrand. I have it still, I was the first man to put up fences. The first camp we put up was a calf camp to stop the calves from taking the milk. I was able to sell cream because I was the transport rider. We used to ride cream for a shilling a can, but we made a profit because in those days there were no shops. We took people's orders and brought them back. We always had a full load. We rode from Gobabis to Ghanzi for cash and from Ghanzi to Maun for cattle. In those days cattle were very cheap. Two and a half pounds in Lobatse was a good price. In Ngamiland you could get an ox for a small drum of water, or a knife – a good one. Cattle which are now sixty rand would then have been five rand.

It was a kind of speculation. We took cattle from Maun to Lobatse and smuggled them into South Africa. In those days there was no abattoir.

In the war petrol was scarce and I went to work for the trader Riley in Maun. That was when I married. The whites in Maun do not farm. They are mostly shopkeepers. Ngamiland, Maun, that world . . . if a white man could get a piece of land there he would do very well. Grazing and ploughing are good. Farming is definitely harder in Ghanzi.

We began farming in Ghanzi towards the end of the war. Before the war the farmers put their own beacons [marking their boundaries] where they wanted. Even if it's to hell and gone, he says, 'Look, that is my beacon!' The whole world was open. Between the farms it was anybody's land. Water came from dug wells, wound up with a bucket and chain. People did not need so much water because they had fewer cattle. Four hundred was a lot; if you had fifty you could get by. The life was quite different then. As long as you had meat and milk the world was free, you could go and shoot. With fifty cattle you farmed on.

Now farming in Ghanzi is getting harder every day. The trouble is labour. What can a person do with them? They [the Bushmen] become more irresponsible. In the old days I could buy two hundred oxen and two

Bushmen alone could look after them; they would be in the kraal every night. But today it's hopeless. You can't give them ten to look after. In the early days they didn't know about drink. When I first came to the land there was no such thing as syphilis. They were a clean nation. No T.B. These are recent developments.

People used to trek twice a year. In the winter, August and September, you can't trek, too hot, no rain. People did it much faster than they do now. You went from water to water. Ghanzi to Lehututu took six days. Then, if you were lucky, to Tsana nearby; but sometimes there was no water there and you had to pass by. It took nineteen days there and another twelve back, fast, on horses; altogether a month away.

Nowadays trekking is a picnic. In the old days you got five shillings a head to trek, and out of that you had to pay for the water, and pay the *volk* [the blacks]. You got water from the chiefs. In those days they were very decent. If you got tired, very tired, you looked for the chief and you gave him the cattle and you went and rested. Sometimes they asked for sixpence, sometimes a shilling, just as they felt.

Now I do not trek, I truck. Trucking was started eight years ago by my son-in-law. On a trek a beast will lose up to a hundred pounds in weight and two grades. On a truck he also loses condition, but by that time he is dead.

4

Ghanzi Afrikaners 1973: a domestic description

I

In 1973 a third of the farms on the Ghanzi ridge were owned by absentee landlords. Some of these were South African entrepreneurs, operating individually or as companies, who had bought up land in 1964 when the price was dropped 25 per cent in an attempt to find buyers. Some were 'leading African producers', settled in accordance with government policy to dissolve the racially segregated pattern of freehold land ownership inherited from the colonial period, who had land rights elsewhere and were using the land at Ghanzi as cattleposts (*Botswana Daily News*, 9 February 1967). A few were Afrikaners who had inherited land and were holding on to it despite settlement elsewhere, perhaps intending to return when they had amassed sufficient cattle or capital to farm. The resident farmers were predominantly Afrikaners (thirty-six out of sixty-five households) but also Coloureds (fifteen), blacks (two) and English-speaking whites (twelve). The Coloureds tended to be concentrated to the west of the Ghanzi block, in Xanagas, an adjacent farming area.[1]

The contemporary life style of the resident Afrikaners is the central focus of this chapter. Although most resident farmers are Afrikaans, Afrikaners are very much an overall minority, being less than a tenth of the 1971 farming block population of 4921, the majority of whom are Bushmen.[2]

Because the farms are large, the farmhouses are usually several kilometres apart, though two or three may cluster strategically about a pan which their boundaries intersect. The average distance between houses is at least twelve kilometres, which leaves some households as far as thirty kilometres from their nearest farming neighbours; though they will be closer to Bushman or Kgalagari families.

The roads of the farming block are the rutted truck tracks which have been worn between the houses. They run intimately through people's

40

yards and past the entrances to their houses, necessitating the expected and mutually desired halt for tea or coffee and conversation. There are no telephones and no postal deliveries, though weekly post is brought to the Camp, where it may be collected. The roads are intermittently crossed by gates, part of the extensive fencing that has recently been erected both to demarcate boundaries and to divide the farms into rotational grazing camps. The constant stopping and starting to open and close the gates churns up the sand at these points into dangerously shifting depths, into which the novice driver is bound to subside.

TABLE 2. *Land ownership in Ghanzi and Xanagas farming blocks by ethnic race group,* * *and owners' place of residence, 1973*

	Resident owners		Absentee owners		All owners	
	No.	Average holding (morgen)	No.	Average holding (morgen)	Average holding (morgen)	Percentage area held
English whites	12	23 722.5	4	43 559.6	31 414.5	39.5
Afrikaners	36	8 613.3	15	11 967.4	10 643.3	42.0
Blacks	2	5 107.9	9	13 851.2	12 261.5	11.6
Coloureds	15	5 384.6	0	0	5 384.6	6.9
TOTAL	65	10 549.7	28	17 086.1	12 517.6	100.0

* The classification is racial, save for the important distinction between English- and Afrikaans-speaking whites

TABLE 3 *Population of Ghanzi and Xanagas farming blocks, 1971*

Name and no. of enumeration area		Population	No. of occupied dwellings
Northern farms	02	1643	257
Central farms	03	1247	233
Western farms	04	1022	174
Xanagas farms	05	1009	177
TOTAL		4921	841

Source: *Report on the Population Census 1971* (Gaborone, Central Statistical Office, 1972), part 3, table 6

In the winter months the farm homesteads are identified from afar, across the bleached grasslands or grey leafless scrub, by a cluster of vivid green growth. It is true that as you approach each house the veld becomes more denuded through the incessant grazing of goats and donkeys and cattle coming in to water. But immediately around their houses the Afrikaners establish little green enclaves by means of constant watering, sometimes by an elaborate irrigation system; more usually by intensive Bushman labour with buckets and watering cans. Here grow tall evergreen citrus trees, the fruit like Christmas illuminations in the dark foliage. There are incongruous small, damp squares of lawn, edged with beds of salvia, geraniums, mesembrianthemum and hollyhock. They say that, given water, anything will grow, and their kitchen gardens vouch for this: tomatoes, lettuce, peas, beans, bananas, paw-paws and melons, surrounded by high hedges of prickly pear, a spiny fruit-bearing cactus. Not every woman is diligent about provisioning her family in this way, and for many years families were too mobile to establish extensive gardens. Before the introduction of borehole and pump, water supplies were fickle even on the advantageous ridge, with rainfall extremely localised, and people and their cattle moving constantly to find the fullest pans, the greenest grazing. They were also much occupied with riding transport.

The careful cultivation of gardens suggests a pride in the appearance of things which other aspects of Afrikaner domestic life belie. The immediate vicinity of each house is littered with the accumulated paraphernalia of ranching life: obselete equipment, pieces of windpumps and butter churns, ox carts, derelict trucks, empty petrol drums, chains, rusting engine blocks, worn-out tyres, and the bleached horns of slaughtered cattle, on which chickens may roost, while guinea fowl and peacocks ('We keep them for their prettiness') scratch and nestle in the fine dust. Bullocks, heifers, cows and oxen stand and stare morosely through the slack strands of fencing wire. Bushman children sit astride gates and fencing posts, Bushman women squat in the yard beside iron cauldrons, smouldering fires, or zinc baths of nuts, mealies or washing. There are mounds of *tsamma* melons stock-piled for chicken and cattle feed, and stout wooden hoppers, Batawana style, filled with ripe, hard corn on the cob. The galvanised corrugated iron dam, filled daily by the pump, stands close to the house attracting a constant stream of bucket-carrying Bushman children and women. Bushman children armed with gut-bound catapults made from discarded truck-tyre inner tubes linger by the dam, hunting the *quelea* finches which are attracted to the spilt water. The constant fire, burning in a detached brick oven at the back of the house to heat water for the farmer's household, meets the continuous needs of other Bushmen for a light for their pipes and provides the fire in which the children roast the small birds they have shot. Within five hundred yards of the water tank will be a scattering of Bushman and other workers' dwellings, built in a variety of traditions and transitions, from the frail

42

Bushman *werf* to the corrugated iron shack, a rusting symptom of modernisation.

This disregard for the appearance of things is a part of culture borne by
a community too intimate for conspicuous consumption. Every man's
economic position, like his life history, is known to everyone else, and the
life style of the rich resembles closely the life style of the poor. The same
taste dictates the manner in which the interiors of the houses are furnished, with polished concrete or linoleum-covered floors, upon which
zebra and goat skins jostle with hand-hooked rugs and squares of mass-
produced floral carpeting from the factories of South West Africa and the
Transvaal. On the walls there are paintings of African sunsets by local
people, framed prints of the Voortrekker monument, symbol of triumphant ascendancy of Afrikanerdom in South Africa, biblical texts in
Dutch, illuminated with cut-out tinfoil flowers, certificates of good
behaviour issued by the school in favour of sons and daughters now grown
up, photographs of the Springbok rugby team, and family portraits of
unsmiling ancestors, straight-backed and straight-laced, staring out of the
same heavy oval frames that are to be found on the walls of thousands of
little houses in black locations throughout southern Africa. In the glass-
fronted display cabinets are hand painted ostrich eggs, African carvings,
miniature bottles of drink, matchbox souvenirs of nights in distant South
African hotels, peacock feathers, china ornaments and tumblers decorated with risqué transfers. There are racks of hunting guns. On the chairs
and couches are soft fur *karosses* – Nama-style blankets of jackal and fox
pelts – beside finely crocheted antimacassars, knitted blankets, patch-
work cushions and minutely embroidered cloths, the accumulated loving
care of older housewives. Younger households have houses that are
accordingly barer.

The decorative accretions of the settled Afrikaner home tend to be
dictated by sentiment and accident rather than any attempt at style or
'taste', though the intrusion of a draped fishing net in one living room
betrayed new influences. The resident English-speaking households are
drawn more explicitly to the common Western suburban housing norm,
communicated in newspapers and periodicals, and experienced in visits
away from Ghanzi which they make with greater frequency than
Afrikaners. The Afrikaners, like the Coloureds, established their idiom
in the isolated interior, governed by principles of stark utility rather than
competitive display. Among Afrikaners a man is not yet valued for his
possessions, nor is there yet any attempt at social discrimination on the
basis of wealth. Poverty is too recent a recollection for most to be any
cause for shame.

In size and complexity the Afrikaner houses varied from a corrugated
iron lean-to up against an unbaked clay room to a substantial brick and

43

stone farmhouse with several rooms, surrounded on three sides by a traditional elevated *stoep*. Some houses have been fitted with sophisticated plumbing. In others water is drawn by hand from the dam, and a rudely screened pit serves as a latrine. Most houses fall between these extremes. All were owner-built for at this level there is little specialisation in Ghanzi; everyone can build, repair trucks and pumps, sink wells and construct dams. The landless few offer their skills in these fields to others, for cash or cattle or grazing rights, but on a limited scale. Most of the houses in 1973 were in the process of being rebuilt, extended and altered, partly because houses are constantly adapted to changing family size and needs, partly because of the wave of affluence the community was then experiencing as a consequence of steadily rising beef prices. Most alterations employed concrete blocks, easily produced locally with sand and Bushman labour, and less wasteful of effort than the fired clay bricks which people had used earlier, deploying the knowledge of indigenous potters to indicate local sources of clay, and building the green bricks into a kiln, which was fired for a week. 'If you make thirty thousand you'll get fifteen thousand good ones; the others will be raw or burned. But the more you make, the higher the proportion of successful ones.'

Ethnic group is strikingly associated with wealth in Ghanzi. The English-speaking whites are significantly wealthier than Afrikaners, Coloureds or blacks, with an average land-holding of 31 415 morgen, to the Afrikaners' 10 643, and the Coloureds' 5 385. The residual blacks are Herero, Kgalagari and Tswana, and in 1973 there were only nine of them. Their average holding in Ghanzi is a little above the Afrikaner average, at 12 262 (see table 2, p. 41).

The history of land-holding in Ghanzi suggests that the returns on farming have to be good to hold the English-speaking farmers, whereas Afrikaners and Coloureds and blacks, with their deeper attachment to place, and their longer conditioning to arid subsistence living standards, are content with the lower return that a smaller holding yields. There is some evidence of anglicisation as a consequence of successful pastoral entrepreneurship. Several of the richer families who now send their children to English-speaking schools are of Afrikaner descent. Perhaps the rationalisation of life style of these successful few extends to changed ethnic identity in calculated conformity with their economic and political interests. The black elite, conditioned by the South African experience, tend to persist in seeing Afrikaners as threatening. Most Afrikaners remain deeply rooted in their received culture which has for so long proved a viable framework for life in the interior, and are deeply attached to that identity as sharers in that culture. Yet pressure to modify the received traditions are relentlessly upon them as the new technology puts participation in the cash and capital economy within their reach.

II

The long tradition of contained economic self-sufficiency persists into the new cash economy, presenting Afrikaners with constant choice, to make or to buy. This is nowhere more apparent than in the intimate domestic economy where the older Afrikaner women tend to cling to former patterns of self-reliance, while the younger ones are attracted to newer patterns of cash-dependent consumption – tinned foods, imported toiletries and mass-produced clothes and furnishings.

Many women make soap, rendering down the fat of pigs, sheep or game, in vast cauldrons over open fires. The recipe embodies the practised skill of generations:

> The harder the fat, the better the soap. Almost any fat will do, but not from an ostrich. A lion makes very good soap . . . the cold water method is good because it's quick and it does not smell. If the soap is going to be good it will be hard in an hour. If you take the *kaaings* [brownings, small pieces of crisp unrendered fat] you can make it up again for soap to give to your Bushmen.

Soap is made partly for use, partly for exchange. It is given to local Bushmen, both workers and seasonal visitors, who bring in exchange fruit in season from the veld, particularly *marama* nuts (actually a legume), whose slightly bitter almond-like flavour enhances cakes and biscuits. There are also more curious items – the *kalkoentjie* ('little turkey'), the *klapper* ('The klapper is a very delicious thing. I have not been to pick them for a long time, but the Bushmen bring them always when they have been to the northern veld'), and gum (resin) eaten as sweets. ('If it's red, blood red, then it's bitter, you must not eat it. But the colourless ones are very sweet. If it gets hard you throw it on the fire and cover it with ash, and it gets completely soft. The Bushmen crush the hard ones, for sugar.') They also bring *tsamma* and larger sweet green melons ('We used to call them kaffir melons, but we're not allowed to say kaffir; our dictionary is full of kaffir words, kaffir corn, kaffir beer, kaffir sheeting.') Melons are preserved dried in strips, later to be boiled in syrup and eaten with cream ('But the children nowadays only like tinned fruit'). Melon can also be made into *konfyt*, preserved fruit in syrup, whose distinctive delight is the crispness of the fruit, an effect achieved by soaking in lime, gathered as stones from the limestone ridge and fired in a slow dung fire in a shallow pit preparatory to being dissolved for the marinade.

All women know how to make spiced boer sausage, and how to cut meat into thin strips for drying as *biltong*. Most can, and also do, butcher the carcasses of sheep, goats and oxen to their own taste, a judicious distribution of bone so that nobody is forced to have a boneless portion.

Only the elder women know how to make coffee substitute from the roots of the *witgat* trees, which are still to be found growing close to older houses where they were purposefully planted a generation earlier 'when everybody knew about it'. The four-stage process – pounding, sweating, drying and roasting of the root – takes thirteen days. People know that the Bushmen make a similar drink from the seeds of a Kalahari bush which the Afrikaners call *koffiepeel*, and which they eat roasted as nuts. Everybody now prefers imported tea to these indigenous drinks, but the older women remark, philosophically, that if things get bad, they will use the old recipes again.

People make golden syrup from sugar and cream of tartar from the roots of the baobab tree, which is called in Afrikaans 'the cream of tartar tree'. Women's and children's clothes are sometimes made at home, from purchased cloth, but are increasingly bought, as are all men's clothes. Only two men retain the ability to make their own shoes. The arrival in the community of an antique furniture dealer with outlets in South Africa, searching for hand-made pieces, has reversed the incipient shame of some families at their hand-carved *riempie* beds and chairs, with leather thonged surfaces, and the great hardwood chests salvaged from the ox wagons, that serve as cupboards. But it has done nothing to stem the tide of plastic, chrome and vinyl furniture flowing weekly westwards on the returning cattle trucks.

Paradox persists. The same woman who buys all her bread in bulk from Mafeking ('We have never been able to grow bread meal here'), freezing it in her paraffin refrigerator, also grinds her own maize in a traditional Tswana mortar, taking her turn along with Bushman women workers at the one and a half metre long pestle, an activity onomatopoeically described in Afrikaans as *stomp*. In the summer when milk is plentiful women make their own butter; but the pursuit of profit militates against this practice. Some farmers, determined to increase cattle weight and price, prohibit all milking, depriving themselves as well as their black dependents of fresh dairy products. Instead they use tinned milk, and butter imported from South Africa.

Many innovations are intrinsically destructive of traditional structures. Paraffin refrigeration eliminates the old necessity to make the slaughter of an animal the occasion for distribution of meat to neighbours, though the expectation of Bushman workers to receive a portion is still met. Trucks eliminate the necessity for hospitality, and render the older pattern of overnight camping around the church for *nagmaal*, the Lord's supper, an anachronism, increasingly replaced by hurried commuter journeying. At the same time, motor transport facilitates visiting between widely scattered households; but the visits are brief, often not long enough for a shared meal. 'It is all hurry, hurry, hurry these days', sighed an old woman whose standards were formed in the leisurely days of donkey transport. Diminished hospitality means diminished obligation. Steadily the bonds of community are pared down to dimensions suited to twentieth-century technology and the market economy, subtly resisted in practices like that of pressing on departing visitors *padkos*, food for the road, and in the insistence that meat must be given, not sold. 'A person can't sell meat.'

Ready availability of cash affects but does not determine the choice to retain traditional ways. However, lack of cash forces the persistence of old patterns, even among the young. The consequent tendency for the poor consistently to be the bearers of the traditional Afrikaner culture (though not all traditionalists are poor) probably detracts further recruits to tradition among the younger generation. The high correlation between commercial failure and traditional culture results in the somewhat irrational perception of cultural innovation as an index of commercial success. The anglicisation of some of the successful farmers reinforces this view. The fact that Coloureds tend to be poor, and hence to retain pre-cash practices, lends the older transitions a further complicating stigma.

The younger generation is more decisively lured from the older pattern by formative years spent in schools in South Africa and South West Africa, where Afrikaners are well advanced on the modernising path (Adam 1971:172–81). The necessity of literacy was lightly experienced by the older generation, who generally learned to read from their parents or random years in short-lived farm schools. Increasingly with the passing of years the necessity for a more systematic and rigorous education was pressed, sometimes by and sometimes on the authorities, though it was not until 1954 that a government-subsidised boarding school for whites was established in Ghanzi, racially segregated in line with prevailing colonial practice.

This brought to an end three decades of hired tutors and dissent. A major problem had been the scattered sparse population. 'Every farmer wants a school at his house, and if it cannot be, their children remain uneducated. . . . It is a shame to see little boys and girls growing up like little Bushmen.'[3]

In 1939 an official report, commenting on the education of Europeans in the Protectorate, stressed the necessity of 'education for escape' since 'the Protectorate is at a dead end economically at least as far as the European population is concerned'. It particularly deplored the parents at Ghanzi for 'clinging to traditional habits and methods' and not making 'the necessary adaptations required by this economic revolution'. It noted that Ghanzi children were on average two years retarded in their intelligence quotient ratings, which were considered to be 'symptomatic of the social and educational level of the community' (Malherbe 1939).

The recent re-evaluation of the economic potential of Ghanzi as commercial ranching territory must lead to a reconsideration of the strategy of education for escape, though South Africa might yet be a good place to acquire the business acumen and ambition for successful ranching. Afrikaners themselves select schools in South West Africa for very different reasons: because they are close, because people have relatives living near the schools, because the religious education in the schools is good, because they believe the German influence has led to higher educational standards than in South Africa or Botswana, and finally because all the other children in the schools are sons and daughters of farmers like themselves. In short, the school is seen as an agency for the conservation of Afrikaner culture, while providing an entrée into the changing world beyond Ghanzi. The collective identity of local children is reinforced in their communal journeying to and from school on the back of cattle trucks, each family taking turns at providing transport for the six hundred kilometre return journey.

Most children leaving school leave Ghanzi for wage employment outside Botswana, as teachers, hairdressers, miners, civil servants. A few return to Botswana as transport riders, railwaymen, traders, farm managers, or to help their parents as farmers. Parents contrast the emigration of most of their children with their own experience of growing up in Ghanzi.

The prolonged absence from Ghanzi of all Afrikaner children over the age of seven leads to a depleted *de facto* white population on the farms for most of the year, despite high fertility. For the thirty-one Afrikaans families for which reliable data exist, the average number of children is four. As this figure includes the incomplete families of young parents, completed family size would be well over six. The range of family sizes is from one to eleven. Evidence from family trees drawn up by a past District Commissioner suggests that Afrikaner families are shrinking, possibly by the selective emigration from the district of the more fecund, less prosperous people in the early 1960s. In 1955, during a period of peak population, a particular couple had ten of their eleven children living in Ghanzi, together with their spouses, and fifty-six of their sixty-four grandchildren, of whom forty-three bore the family name – 'Every time you kick a bush out jumps a Swanepoel.' Only nineteen of these eighty-five family members were still living in Ghanzi in 1973, though only the original parents had died.

The English-speaking families are less fecund, with an average of 1.5 children per household. Children might positively deter English-speakers from living in the district.

With the improved transport now readily available (three farmers have light planes which can land fairly easily on dry pans and every farmer has

Fig. 10. The new generation: farmers' children at the stock pens at the quarterly Ghanzi cattle sale

at least one truck), women can now choose to have their babies delivered in hospitals in South or South West Africa, and many do, particularly if their mothers live outside Botswana. Older women were all confined at home in Ghanzi, with the help of trained or untrained midwives. Some women, especially the poorer ones, still have their babies delivered at home with a local midwife living in to assist.

The tradition of self-sufficient medicine remains strong. Every household has its medicine chest with a wide range of patent and prescribed medicines, traditional and modern, and there is a wide range of experience and anecdote on the effectiveness of each. Thus the *Lewenessence: Dr Kiesouw se Beroemde ou Duitse Geneesmiddel* (Essence of Life: Dr Kiesouw's famous old German Healing Agent) 'is an outstanding medicine for fever. I learned of it from an old Englishman who always had a bottle in his pocket.'

The appointment of a doctor to Ghanzi in 1973 was interpreted (realistically) as a service to the blacks rather than whites, though tardy use of his expertise in emergencies was beginning. Earlier a doctor from a mission hospital at Maun, three hundred kilometres to the north, had paid periodic flying visits to Ghanzi, but the infrequency of the service had undermined its usefulness. For major predictable disorders most Afrikaners still travel to private doctors in Windhoek or Johannesburg. Others retain unshaken faith in the efficacy of old remedies, even for such things as appendicitis and broken limbs. These remedies belong to different traditions. One is described as *maphadi* medicine: 'Surely it's a black language word, or maybe Portuguese. It was something the Angola boers knew about.... I heard the other day that in Gobabis they are now trying to stop the *maphadi* doctor.' *Maphadi* includes such bizarre remedies as goat dung in warm wine, and a urine-soaked baby's diaper for the treatment of sore eyes, besides a range of now patented pills and powders. 'In that time you didn't take the tonsils or the appendix out; people got the same sicknesses but they know how to doctor them.'

Several other families follow a natural healing system similar to that recorded in the 1920s by a Mrs Professor J. Kemp of the University College of Potchefstroom. The interest of this system lies in its explicit commendation of what Mrs Kemp called 'kaffir' medical practices, which were considered superior to Western practice. A well-thumbed copy of Mrs Kemp's text serves as the local manual. The system is based on healing through sun, air, clay, steam and a diet of thick soured milk, a Bantu staple in southern Africa. 'The kaffirs put great value on the application of clay treatment.' Thus, for pneumonia, 'We always put clay on the stomach, back and chest. At the most thirty-six applications of clay porridge will be sufficient to master the most serious pneumonia' (Kemp 1920:81–7). Mrs Kemp's illustrated book is written in that colloquial Afrikaans which is still spoken in Ghanzi, but which is being stamped out in South Africa by relentless academic pressure.[4]

III

The Afrikaner year is paced out by seasonal demands, quarterly cattle sales and quarterly church services. The rains in November, February and March mark the time for ploughing and planting a small crop of maize for consumption. After the rains the roads briefly consolidate their surfaces, travel is easy, grazing is plentiful and so is surface water. Released from the necessity to come in to water each day the cattle go wild. April, May and June are good months to move big herds of cattle to the abattoir in Lobatse. April is the month for the innoculation of herds against botulism and other endemic diseases, and for de-horning, to qualify for a bonus at the abattoir.

50

Game is plentiful in the winter, and easier to get in the dry, open winter landscape. June school holidays are the time for week-long hunting expeditions into the veld, for laying in stocks of dried game meat as *biltong*. Game licences are charged on a sliding scale by nationality and ethnic group.[5] Although they pay less than aliens, Afrikaners pay more than local blacks, which gives them cause for grumbling complaint that non-racialism is an inconsistent convenience for the majority. They express their disapproval of the hunting regulations by their frequent violation.

The highlight of the Afrikaner year is the celebration of the New Year, in which the whole community converges on one farm for a day and a night of dancing, drinking, eating, courting and games. The host erects a huge tarpaulin at the place of the festivities, and the guests arrive towards dusk, bringing food with them. There is dancing through the night. Cattle are slaughtered and roasted on open fires, the traditional *braaivleis*. On that day there is horse racing, with no betting, in which the men compete for a cup. It is New Year which housewives anticipate when they redecorate their houses in the equivalent of English spring-cleaning. Christmas, lacking the underpinning of either commercial exploitation or religious ritual, passes almost without notice, except on the company farms where the distribution of meat and liquor to labourers brings all work to a halt for several stupefied days.

Church services are held quarterly when the *dominies* or *predikants* travel from South West Africa to officiate at the quarterly communion services (*nagmaal*) of the two reformed congregations. The *Gereformeerde* or *dopper* congregation, the more fundamentalist and less sophisticated denomination, meets in the converted *stoep* of a house in D'Kar, forty kilometres east of the Camp. The *Nederduitse Gereformeerde* congregation, part of the original established church of the Cape, has a church building in the Camp. Built in 1954 it is a solid, stolid unimaginative structure of bricks under a corrugated iron roof, squatting in its fenced enclosure amidst the sparse Kalahari scrub. Here four times a year the white worshippers come with their usual Bushman retinue: men to open the cattle gates, women and children who come for the outing and expect in return to makes fires for cups of tea, and meals for the few who still choose to camp out overnight between the *nagmaal* services. The church grounds are purposely large to accommodate the many families who used to camp before the truck made commuting possible.

The deacons and elders of the church dress formally, distinctively, like the *dominie*, in black suits, white dress shirts and white bow ties. During the service they sit apart, in front of the congregation, symbolically between the *dominie* and the people. The others dress carefully in their best. All the women wear hats. The little girls wear pink and white and green crocheted shawls, bright floral dresses, and stiff white organdie hats decorated with artificial flowers. Some women wear black, but most wear cotton floral dresses of decent length, with stockings. The hymns and psalms are sung unaccompanied in measured, heavy, sonorous tone. On a Sunday in 1973 they sang,

> Let us take up our cross with joy.
> Your father's heart knows all our troubles,
> You hear our sighs and our complaints.

and the *dominie* took as his text, 'For you brought nothing into the world.' He warned the congregation against the fickle security of earthly riches, reminding them of unpredictable changes of fortune in times past. Afterwards a woman said, 'Don't you love our *predikant*? When he preaches you really feel it in your heart.'

Until they are seven, old enough to be sent away to school, children stay at home in the constant care of their parents, who, although helped by Bushmen in this task, are reluctant to relinquish the sole care of their children to them even for a day. Children accompany their parents everywhere, with none of that regard for regularity of eating and sleeping which is so prominent a part of the English norms for child care. Late at night one will see children sitting quietly beside parents, listening to adult conversation, tracing with their fingers the pattern on an antimacassar, plaiting and unplaiting the fringes of cushion covers, awaiting the bumping ride home in the darkness.

Afrikaners visit one another constantly, not by invitation at pre-arranged times, but in the course of the daily or weekly routines, to borrow equipment, tools, spare parts for the constantly deteriorating trucks, tractors and water pumps; to share news of cattle born, bought or sold, of prices, profits; to deliver or take orders for purchases in Mafeking on the weekly cattle run; to arrange who will fetch the children from school at the next half-term holiday. The slaughter of a pig or ox is the occasion for relations to gather to help in the labour. They will eat meals together between work, and they may stay overnight to help with the butchering, sorting the lean from the fat meat, and cutting up the fat for soap. Pigs are kept purely for soap and the making of small quantities of bacon. 'The Afrikaans people do not eat pigs! It says so in the Bible. The Lord himself filled them with devils and his mark is on their legs.' Visiting is not reserved for weekends, since work and leisure have not yet hardened into discrete categories as in the world of employment. But Sundays are intensely social as people gather for house worship, and stay on to talk, and then to visit those who should have come but did not.

On every occasion children are present. There is no Afrikaner equivalent of the English dinner party from which children are excluded, though there are evening parties, where substantially homely hot meals are served, and people dance to gramophone records or piano-accordion music, while the elderly look on and talk and tend to the young children. Everyone remembers Hettie Roux's wedding as the best party in Ghanzi for a long time. Hettie's parents gave the wedding party, and Hettie's brothers tied tin cans to the springs of the bridal bed, in a room of the mother's house, and the guests stayed and danced all night long.

Before Independence civil servants in the Camp led a legendary social life, with wild parties to which the more anglicised Afrikaners were invited. Independence brought a less frivolous cadre of administrators whose recreations are more earnest and less frantic. 'There used to be a good social life in the Camp – dances, parties at people's houses, hotel dances – now there's bugger all.'

Children are defined as neither a nuisance nor as a special blessing. They are accepted, absorbed into daily routines with a minimum of fuss, to which they respond with quiet confidence and a remarkable obedience. The whole family may accompany the father when he makes a journey across the Kalahari. A man whose wife was away for two months looked after his three pre-school daughters by taking them with him in the truck wherever he went, camping with them beside the road at night as he journeyed to and from Lobatse.

Relationships with parents, despite this constant intimacy, are those of careful deference. Close physical intimacy must be countered with social distance if age distinctions are to be maintained (van den Berghe 1972). A child never, even in adulthood, addresses its parents in the second person, even though there is in Afrikaans a polite form of the second person, *u* rather than *jy*. Rather they make repetitive use of the term of address. Thus 'May I fetch mother's coat for mother?' The effect is as if the conversation were being conducted through an intermediary, a common African device for establishing status differences. Relationships with mother are more intimate, those with father more distant. It is the mother who hits the children, but father whose disapproval they fear.

The enduring strength of the family as a group of tightly related descendants is reflected in the Afrikaner rule for naming children, which particularly links alternate generations in bonded pairs sharing the same name. Thus the same names are handed down from generation to generation. The eldest son receives the names of his father's father – all of them – while the eldest daughter receives those of her mother's mother. The second son receives the names of his mother's father, the second daughter the names of her father's mother. The third son receives his father's names, the third daughter her mother's names. The naming of subsequent children passes from maternal to paternal kin, in strict alteration and according to sex.

A particular warmth is reserved by a grandparent for the child with whom names are shared. 'He is my own child, this one.' The grandparents' anticipation of thus sharing a name can be so strong that a grandfather deprived of grandsons may insist that a granddaughter receive his names, with or without minor modifications to accommodate gender – hence Willema, Jacoba, Dawida. The third son of a third son will have the same name as his eldest brother; confusion is averted by various devices such as the repetition of the first name, Jan-Jan, or the use of initials pronounced as a name, Eswee for S. W.

The adherence to this particular tradition, with all its implicit social controls – family solidarity, respect for elders, continuity – is a useful indication of the resilience of the community to undermining innovation. Only those who had stepped outside the Afrikaner fold in marrying non-Afrikaners appeared to have dropped the practice. Despite the grumbling at the weight of the string of archaic names which each of their children must inherit (Cornelius Christiaan Stephanus Booisen, Petronella Magdalena Susanna Magrietha), young parents conform to the tradition, contracting names in everyday practice to Chris, Fanie, Grieta, Nell.

Marriage binds the man and woman into a symmetrical kinship system, in which his and her families have an equal place. Maternal and paternal kin are addressed and referred to by the same terms, *ma* for mother and mother-in-law; *pa* for father and father-in-law. Spouses' sisters, like the wives of one's own brothers, are called *skoonsuster*, beautiful sister.

The place of girls is inside the house, of boys outside it. When a girl is old enough to play, a Bushman girl a little older than herself will be detailed to come into the house as her companion. This Bushman child will accompany the family on outings and will have access to all the places to which the child has access, in the special role of retainer rather than as equal. Nevertheless the relationship becomes intimate. It is in this way that Afrikaners become so fluent in various Bushman languages, and say with conviction, 'We know the Bushmen, we grew up with them.'

Bonds established in childhood persist throughout life. There are links between particular boer and Bushman families, paired at each age and sex, through this institution. A Bushman woman said,

> I went to work for the de Wets when I was little. I was Annie de Wet's *matie* [playmate]. She is a year younger than me. My father worked for her father. I grew big with them. When they moved to Mafeking I moved with them. Annie always said, 'When I'm grown up and I get a man and marry him you must come and work for me.' So I did. She married a policeman in South West. I'm trying to get a passport to go there. They are very good people. When they cook

food, they serve themselves and then they serve you the same food. The man is naughty. He hits people but he never hits me. If you work for them they look after you. You don't walk naked. And at the end of the month you get money.

The boy's place is outside the house. At an early age the Afrikaner boy is assigned a Bushman playmate with whom he is encouraged to explore the world outside, physical and social. The Bushman receives food, second-hand clothes, and occasional small cash payments for his services. Forays into the veld are made with other Bushman boys on donkeys, later on horses. Every man can ride. From an early age boys will take guns with them, to shoot game. Men recall with pride the tender age at which they shot their first lion or wildebeest.

By contrasting her restriction to the house with her brother's freer access to the world outside, a girl absorbs not only her female economic role but her symbolic role as keeper of the intimate, the one to whom the task of preservation through exclusion has been entrusted. A woman who rejects her feminine role is derided as a *mannetjiesvrou*, a little man-woman, defined as 'one who instead of working inside the house works outside it'. The implication that there is a deep sexual division of labour centred about household tasks is not readily observable. Although men never go into the kitchen to prepare food, women drive trucks, handle guns, slaughter animals and run trading stores, without incurring apparent ostracism. The singling out of particular woman as *mannetjiesvrou* seems arbitrary. Yet the symbolic association of the women with the inside of the house persists. Access to the inside of the house is carefully restricted. The rule seems to be that those who come inside the house are those with whom all intimacies are permissible. By corollary, exclusion from the inside of the house is exclusion from the group. It is in these terms that a woman was scandalised by the behaviour of a local black tax official, who walked unbidden into her house instead of stopping at the furnished *stoep*, which, being neither inside nor outside, serves as an appropriate place to receive marginal guests such as high status outsiders. This rule gives added significance to the behaviour of another family who invited the visiting black *dominie* into their house for a meal.

Domestic servants are of a marginal category who although not of the group have access to the intimate interior of the house. Their social incorporation strikingly parallels this physical access. Always female, invariably Bushman, they are the group from whom the Afrikaner men recruit mistresses. This behaviour and its implications must be seen against the broader framework of relationships between Afrikaners, Bushmen and other ethnic groups.

A domestic description

Extract from transcript of tape recording, Ghanzi, 1973

Speaker: Coloured (Afrikaans-speaking) woman, aged 65
   Occupation: farmer
   Widow, adult children
   Place of birth: Cape, South Africa
   Citizenship: Motswana
   Land owned: 5000 morgen

My father's family came from South West Africa originally. My father's
father was from overseas, a Scot. My mother's mother was Coloured. They
were cattle, sheep and goat farmers. When my grandfather died my father
and his brothers moved to Rietfontein in the northern Cape. We came to
Lehututu in 1915 from Rietfontein, to trade cattle with the shopkeepers.
That was the only outlet. We were a little group who came up together, and
later came through to Olifantskloof together. My oldest sister married Jan
Villiers in Lehututu before we left, and they came too. My family did not
mind when my sister married a white man; this family we knew very well
from ages back in South Africa. The Viljoens also trekked up with us from
the Cape to Lehututu. Later when my sister Anna married the Viljoens' son,
they [Viljoens] were cross, very cross. But before they treated us as their
family. We were very much in contact with them from the beginning. There
were no whites in Lehututu, just the traders, one of whom took a black wife,
and the Kalaharis and the Viljoens.

In 1921 my father came to Ghanzi, and in 1924 he moved to Olifantskloof.
In those days it was just veld. We had a great struggle for water. There was a
spring at Olifantskloof where my father wanted to settle and make a farm,
but his three wells yielded almost no water. Because of water we moved here,
where previously Hereros had lived. My father opened up their old wells and
got water. Now we have, besides wells, fifteen boreholes and almost no
water. The borehole at the house pumps dry in fifteen minutes, but it fills
quickly enough to meet household needs. I can only water the vegetables
every fourth day. We have three hundred cattle.

I married a German soldier in 1931, but he died in 1937. [A contemporary
says: 'He was a Prussian and very wild. He swore at everybody and he had
no respect for anybody, but he loved animals. He blasphemed like mad. One
day he scratched his face and developed face cancer. He died penitent, saying
he'd always tempted God to strike him, and now He had struck him. He
knew He existed.'] I moved to my father's farm. My father had got a little bit
of freehold in Ghanzi and he moved there in 1938, where he died in 1944.
When I got the chance of buying this farm very cheaply, I did. I haven't paid
it off yet.

There was always apartheid, but when I was a child you didn't feel it so

56

terribly as you do today. In those days we had many more friends. As a child in South Africa we were more friendly with whites, free house visiting, we had more traffic with whites. Apartheid was something the whites developed later. There was always a difference between races, call it inferiority, or colour, or whatever, but I must be truthful and say that in my heart I also have apartheid. At least I keep to my own kind. In my parents' house we were taught only to mix with our own kind, and that is how we are. There are certain families in Ghanzi that are never *snaaks* [peculiar] towards me. The apartheid is there, it is true, but if I go into certain households there is never any funny attitude towards me personally. Most of those people were delivered by my mother. There were no doctors at that time. I don't want to be despised, but I don't feel it, because you see I've got my feelings of apartheid.

The Tswana government has made a difference. I can't explain it. But there were certain things that one got used to under the British that have now altered, but we do our best to fit in with the new life. When the school got integrated, in the beginning it naturally was – we weren't scared, no, but a person feels most at home with his own kind. In the early years our children had teachers who were the same race as ourselves.

I am born in Africa; but they impress on us that we are not Afrikaners, that we are Coloureds. Take our origins. My father's father was a Scot, my mother's father was a Scot. One married an Engelbrecht, Coloured. The other also married a Coloured, not Nama, but mixed blood. We have always been Afrikaans-speaking, but we wouldn't call ourselves Afrikaners because we are not white. It's a very emotional matter, because you are not responsible for your existence. Take my children. Their father is white, I married a white. Only one sister of ours married a Coloured, but our children are going back. This living together [non-racialism] is pushing them back. We accept it. We have learned to accept everything. I am old now. I accept peacefully everything now.

5

Preserving boundaries: similarities, ambiguities and avoidances

I

It has been suggested that we can find clues to a people's social structure by looking at the paradigms implicit in the classificatory order they impose on the natural world confronting them. A telling image which occurs constantly in Afrikaner accounts is that of a multiplicity of juxtaposed 'worlds' each inhabited by an appropriate species. Thus Ghanzi is 'a lion's world' and also 'a cattle world', but not 'a sheep's world' – 'Down in the south near Nossop, that is a sheep's world.' South is also 'a Hottentot's world', whereas Ghanzi is 'a Bushmen's world'. Ghanzi is itself a world in contrast to 'South West', Ngamiland, or even, laughingly, apologetically, in an unguarded moment, to Botswana itself. 'Here is Ghanzi's world, there is Botswana.'

Appropriate species can share a world: goats, zebra and eland run with the cattle on the farm veld. Amongst people, a single species with the potential for miscegenation, close juxtaposition of different kinds can be dangerous since social order is seen to rest on the conservation of prevailing identities and boundaries. Thus whites and blacks alike are seen to have a disastrous impact on local Bushmen by disturbing a social order in which the different groups had retained their distinctiveness.

> Earlier days the Bushmen were absolutely divided. Here there were the Makoko, in the middle were the Nharo, south were the !Xo, and such. Now they are all mixed up and it's bad.

> In the early days they did not know about drink. When I first came into the land there was no such thing as syphilis. They were a clean nation.

> They are a nation going backwards not forwards. The little men themselves, you'll never find him taking a black woman or anything

58

like that, but the blacks are very fond of taking their women. They are bastardising themselves out of existence.

Existence outside secure ethnic identity is no existence at all. Intermarriage carries grave consequences for every group. 'The Lord himself created the nations of the world, the Makoko nation, the Afrikaner nation, the Damara nation. . . . Now the Lord made us different. Why? Why did the Lord make different languages and nations?' Ethnic distinctions are sacredly legitimated in a god-given heterogeneous social order. The ordered universe is one in which each has his place, not in some hierarchy of power and privilege, but horizontally, in a pattern of juxtapositions. The imagery may be as naive and anachronistic as that of the flat earth, limitless, with space on its horizons for those with the determination to reach them; but it is important to see that this is indeed the model, for its implications are very different from those of the hierarchical model dominant in Western conceptions. Social order is seen to rest on the maintenance of proper relationships between clearly defined groups. It is only when there is this clarity that social relationships can be established. They are of course not necessarily relationships between equals.

II

The Ghanzi Afrikaners see themselves as belonging to a particular segment of Afrikanerdom. They call themselves *Kalahari boere*, thereby drawing attention both to their unique environment, the 'thirstland', which demands its own particular cultural adaptations, and to their relationship to the means of production. A boer is not a wage labourer. He may be a subsistence nomadic pastoralist or a peasant, or a commercial producer for the agricultural market. He is always independent, with control over his means of subsistence. Minimally he has a *plaas*, the meaning of which is frequently violated by the English translation 'farm'. Afrikaners themselves reserve the word *boerdery* to describe the activities of commercial production. Ghanzi Afrikaners stress that while they have always had a *plaas*, they have only recently started *boerdery*.

At the same time they see themselves belonging to a more inclusive category which embraces all Afrikaners. On the walls of their houses they hang the customary symbols of Afrikaner identity: pictures celebrating epic moments in the history of nineteenth-century Afrikanerdom, photographs of that emotive symbol, the Voortrekker monument in Pretoria and, on one occasion, a carefully framed pamphlet distributed in the 1930s in South Africa, urging on Afrikaners the exclusive use of the Afrikaans language in private and public at all times.[1] Against this must

Fig. 11.1 Common law widow of white farmer: white father, Bushman mother, speaking only Nharo
Fig. 11.2. Bushman worker
Fig. 11.3. Afrikaner farmer
Fig. 11.4. Herero aristocrat, daughter of a Ghanzi land owner

Fig. 11.5. Old G/wi man visiting the farms from the veld
Fig. 11.6. Coloured man, Ghanzi Camp
Fig. 11.7. Afrikaner cattle drover. (Reproduced by permission of Argus Africa News Service, Cape Town)

61

immediately be placed the newer political identity, 'I am a Motswana.' When the Independence of Botswana in 1966 forced a choice of political identity, all Ghanzi Afrikaners rapidly perceived the advantages of Botswana citizenship, and supported Khama's Democratic Party.

Many writers have noted the fissiparous tendency of the trekkers in the interior in the nineteenth century. Few as they are, and despite the complex bonds of kinship which unite almost all of them with all others – indeed, perhaps because of them[2] – Ghanzi Afrikaners appear to be divided, principally on the basis of religious denomination. The two Afrikaner denominations with congregations in Ghanzi are the established mother church from the Cape, the *Nederduitse Gereformeerde* church, and the fundamentalist nineteenth-century schism, the *Gereformeerde* or *dopper* church. The former has a public image of liberal enlightenment; the latter is the church of the pastoral rural hinterland. (Neither should be confused with the third Dutch Reformed church in South Africa, the *Hervormde Kerk* of the Transvaal, nineteenth-century republican rival of the Established church of the Cape.)

The two Afrikaner churches in the farming area are, as they say, sister churches, in communion with one another, which means that the two congregations are expected and encouraged to attend one another's services. Their cooperation in Ghanzi probably exceeds that characterising sister churches in more populated places, in the same way that denominational differences are often minimised in beleaguered mission fields.

Nevertheless denominational identity remains quite distinct. A *Gereformeerde* woman drew our attention to the informal yet persistent segregation of denominations at the joint service held in the *Nederduitse Gereformeerde* church, one sitting on the right side of the central aisle, the other on the left. 'I don't know why we do it, we always sit so.' Spatially in the farming block there is a similar clustering by denomination, with the *Gereformeerdes* east of the *Nederduitse Gereformeerdes*. Proximity is a consequence and a cause of dense denominational social networks, strongly reinforced with kinship ties. In the 1930s the small flourishing farm school at Kgoutsa in the west was on the farm of a *Nederduitse Gereformeerde* family. Several *Gereformeerde* families, with farms and pasturage in the east, petitioned government assistance to start a second school 'on our side' at D'Kar, since Kgoutsa, forty kilometres away, was 'too far for our children to attend school there and live at home', and 'the boarding there is too high for us'.[3] The solicited opinion of the Kgoutsa schoolmaster, an outsider, on the matter was that these were simply excuses, since 'religion plays a great part in their antipathy to this school, because they are bound to a different church and they expect that most of the school time has to be spent on religion'.[4] In the same year

Fig. 12. *A visit by Pieter Retief and his escort to the Zulu king Dingaan*. This framed print on the wall of a farmhouse symbolises the Afrikaners' continuing concern with their historical origins and their identity

a magistrate visiting from Maun addressed the farmers on the question of the school, appealing to them 'to put aside differences amongst yourselves and cooperate'. He urged full attendance at the Kgoutsa school, which he described as 'not good . . . the school building is badly equipped and the teachers' quarters a disgrace'. Nevertheless, 'Education must be carried on.'[5]

The division between the two denominations at this time may well have been exacerbated by what the schoolmaster in 1934 had called 'the bastard question',[6] since by the 1930s several of the sons of poorer *Gereformeerde* families had set aside the customary racial boundary to marry the eligible daughters of neighbouring Coloured fellow believers.

III

Barth has suggested that it is by concentrating on the processes of exclusion and inclusion which define and maintain boundaries that our understanding of the nature and functioning of ethnicity will be heightened. The events in Ghanzi in the 1930s, as the community responded to the intermarriage of Afrikaners and Coloureds, offer evidence of this kind, though it is inevitably somewhat distorted by recollections pressed and repressed by four decades of increasing awareness and sensitivity to the political potency of race. It seems clear, nonetheless, that some *Gereformeerdes* had already embarked upon redefining their identity in purely cultural terms, not only in Ghanzi, but also at Molepolole in the eastern Protectorate, where 'practically the whole European population' was reported to be involved in 'the problem' of 'race mixture' (Malherbe 1939).

> The difficulty lies in the fact that the people with Coloured blood are as respectable and on practically the same economic level as the Europeans. Consequently they have their children in the same school as Europeans. . . . The practical difficulty lies in the fact that just recently one of the fairly large European families has become linked up by marriage with one branch of the Coloured family. . . . They are therefore objecting to the exclusion of these half-Coloured children from the school.

Ghanzi Afrikaners had experienced similar pressures for racial segregation, both from within the community and from influential outsiders. In 1931 the new schoolmaster hired to teach the *Gereformeerde* children on the eastern farms had 'found that his school was a sort of a family or private school and that bastards were included. He refused to admit the bastards.'[7] Racial rather than cultural segregationist practice prevailed. The 'bastards' were served by a succession of tutors, privately hired for fourteen head of young heifers a year, until official British planning legitmated their exclusion by supporting a small school amidst the farms at Xanagas, some 160 kilometres west of Ghanzi, where Coloureds, and those whites who had contracted marriages with non-white wives, were encouraged to settle. This became the recognised place for Coloured education.

For many years conditions at Xanagas school troubled parents. One of the more articulate British parents complained that 'the Coloured children in the Bechuanaland Protectorate . . . mostly direct or indirect descendants of old British pioneers, including government officials . . . are growing up heathens'. He described Xanagas boarding conditions where 'all eleven children sleep on the floor in one room'.[8] Conditions for whites were not any better. Many children had neither tutors nor schooling. Others, boarded out with families near the Kgoutsa school 'had to be content to sleep on the floor of the dining room . . . the diet was most monotonous and deficient . . . the whole atmosphere was demoralising and ennervating' (Malherbe 1939).

The realisation in 1947 of *Gereformeerde* ambitions for their own school at D'Kar did not mean any basic improvement in standards of living or education.

> The school has a grass roof and the insects are busy eating the grass, continually a rain of wood powder is falling on the children and the books. The school has three windows made of wood and on a stormy day it is impossible to live here. . . . In the rainy season the walls can fall down . . . nearly all the children suffer from malaria.[9]

Boarding of children was still necessary because of the dispersal of households and the absence of motor transport. 'Nine boys and girls sleep together in the same room. . . . These nine children have to cook for themselves, the main dish is porridge, bread and *biltong*. Everyone can see these children are underfed.' The children, now adult, look back on their schooldays with stereotyped nostalgia. 'We had to cook for ourselves and milk our own cows. In the mornings we had quickly to make *pap* [ground maize porridge] and tidy our beds and then walk nearly two miles to school. When we came home we had to make *pap* again and collect firewood. . . . It was a decent school, really.'

The building of a new white boarding school in Ghanzi Camp in 1954 by the government brought to an end the denominational separation of schools. But the old anxieties about religious doctrine and colour lingered, festering, leading to instances of the sudden withdrawal of pupils and staff from the school. In January 1963 the school had been unable to open on time because the teaching staff had shrunk to one. The pupils had likewise dwindled from a hundred to thirty, due to 'friction among farmers, family feuds and petty squabbling' (*Mafeking Mail*, 7 February 1964). When towards the end of that same year the government intention to desegregate all schools was made known,[10] the Afrikaner community came together all concerted outrage and protest, internal dissensions forgotten in the face of external threat.

The emotionally overwrought discussion at the public meeting called by the District Commissioner as chairman of the school board in November 1963, exposes the Afrikaner perception of this threat, a curiously contradictory blend of fear of assimilation ('What sort of a mixed nation will be brought about if children go to school together?') and its apparent opposite, the heightening of ethnicity through contact ('Children will concentrate on racial affairs instead of school work', 'Such mixing will drive the races further apart').[11] Much was also made of how the government had lured them away from their old private schools into the state system, only to impose this unacceptable condition upon them.

Underlying the publicly expressed disquiet at the proposed 'mixing with natives' was the more immediate, familiar and unvoiced alarm at sharing school with Coloureds. For the government ruling on school desegregation had embraced a qualifying cultural factor, which would in practice have debarred the vast majority of local blacks from qualifying even supposing they were wanting the experience: all children admitted to English medium, as opposed to Tswana medium, schools had to be proficient in English. Despite their reluctance, the Afrikaners, like the Coloureds, were much closer to the English-speaking world than were the blacks.

The only child to register for admission at Ghanzi under the new conditions, in December 1963, was a Coloured child of one of the 'bastards'. The immediate threat of school desegregation was proximity to the very people who had for the past thirty years presented so peculiar a threat to the local community, their very own Coloured kinsmen.

IV

Analytically the anxiety aroused in Afrikaners by the prospect of this close juxtaposition is not surprising. Given the premise that ethnic identity matters to a particular group, it will be those who most acutely threaten that identity who will be avoided. Bushmen, with their highly distinctive appearance, culture and life style, can be admitted to all kinds of intimacy without ethnic confusion; as workers, household members, fellow travellers. Blacks are likewise distinctive. The idea of boundaries between blacks and Afrikaners or Bushmen and Afrikaners being blurred or ambiguous is scarcely imaginable. But Coloureds are very like boers, the more so when they are first generation descendants of boers. If Afrikaner distinctiveness is to be maintained, there must be a rigid exclusion of Coloureds from intimacy, a total avoidance of situations where boers might become indistinguishable from Coloureds. The necessity for the severe policing of this particular boundary is evidenced in the ease with which liaisons are established across it.

A more tolerable and less threatening ambiguity arises on the boundary between the racially close English-speaking whites. Whereas assimilation to Coloureds threatens the community with depressed social status, and the individual with exclusion, assimilation to the English, though entailing a certain exclusion from the community, offers the individual enhanced opportunities for social advancement. It also offers the Afrikaner community links with those sophisticated in administrative and financial negotiations. In the Protectorate the distinction between

English- and Afrikaans-speaking whites has never formally been recognised, though informally there has always been an awareness of the
distinctiveness of Afrikaners, ideal pioneers, 'people who can walk about
with their shirts hanging out of holes in their trousers . . . rough types.
They may be difficult people to handle, they may be difficult people to
deal with, but they are the people who will be able to tame that land.'[12]
English settlers have been a small but powerful part of the Ghanzi
settlement from its inception. It is curious how sharp the boundary
between the groups remains, how few ambiguities arise despite intermarriage and how there is 'flow of personnel across the boundaries' (Barth
1969:23).

We might see Ghanzi Afrikaners' identity as a clustering of discrete
criteria, none by itself sufficient to confer group membership, but in
conjunction decisively defining membership. These criteria are language
(which must be Afrikaans), physical appearance (white skin, caucasian
features), biological descent (European parentage, which implies European grandparentage too), and religion (all Afrikaners in Ghanzi are
expected to belong to one of the two Dutch Reformed churches). Beyond
these key criteria is a residual category of cultural features, including
distinctive patterns of diet, subsistence, kinship and recreation, which are
recognised as transient: absence of these features cannot disqualify one
from group membership, but their display will signal possible group
membership. Although ethnic groups cannot be culturally defined, since
ethnic identities outlive changing cultural patterns (Barth 1969:4–9), the
closeness or looseness of the fit between group and culture is itself of
interest. The looseness of fit suggests the intrinsic irrelevance of particular cultural features, though their simultaneous presentation tends to
constitute identity. Each particular cultural feature shared with a neighbouring ethnic group represents, postively, a basis for interaction and
shared interests, and negatively, a threat of assimilation.

Language is the most central criterion of Afrikaner group membership,
yet not all those whose mother tongue is Afrikaans are counted as
Afrikaners. Afrikaans is also the home language of most Coloureds, who
neither count themselves nor are counted by Afrikaners. 'I am born in
Africa; but they impress on us that we are not Afrikaners, that we are
Coloureds.'

The position of those who are born into Afrikaans families but who
switch group allegiance by changing their home language is viewed with
particular contempt. 'If you are so rotten that you abandon your own
mother tongue, you are good for nothing.' Anglicised Afrikaners are
called *baster Engels*, bastard Englishmen. Because in the Afrikaner
experience the English have invariably been the powerful, anglicisation is
despised as toadying. An Afrikaans woman who married an English

settler in Ghanzi in the 1930s is reputed never to have spoken a word of English to him all her life. He for his part spoke only English, and thus, unilingually, they passed their life happily together. Their children became English. The ostensible inability of local Afrikaners to speak English contrasts with their facility in all other local languages: Tswana, Kgalagari, Herero, Makoko, Nharo, Nama and less commonly G/wi. A retiring District Commissioner in the 1960s warned his successor not to let the local farmers delude him into the misconception that they were unable to speak English as most of them were fairly fluent.[13] Their vehement denial of this fluency suggests deliberate insulation from non-Afrikaner whites.

In 1973 a white English Magistrate, presiding over a court session in Ghanzi at which an inordinate amount of interpretation had proved necessary – from and into Tswana, English, Herero, and what was ignorantly and contemptuously referred to as 'Bushman' – singled out the Afrikaners for particular complaint at their persistence in talking a language not officially recognised in the land. Afrikaner familiarity with many indigenous languages was overlooked, despite several incidents during the hearings in which Afrikaners and other witnesses were clearly outpacing the interpreters in their mutual understanding of one another's evidence, while the English Magistrate appeared the unilingual outsider.

While white skin and European features now seem to be essential prerequisites for Afrikaner group membership, this was not always so. In the 1930s and 1940s cultural factors outweighed racial factors in Ghanzi. A child of a Coloured/white marriage, contracted in this period, recalls from his childhood the closeness of his bonds with his white cousins. 'Our house was their house, we grew up together.' As fellow believers, members of white and Coloured *Gereformeerde* households 'used to come together to sing psalms, sometimes at Driefontein, sometimes at Groenhof, sometimes at Weltevreden'. One of the Coloured wives would accompany them on the organ. 'She had been brought up by the Germans in South West and she knew how to play music, not by the ear but by the notes.' There were a lot of parties. 'It's only later they got proud, superior. It was after my father died. While my father was alive we were very close, but when he died they kept themselves apart.'

The passing of time loosened the bonds of kinship as a new and more distantly related generation grew up. The immigration of the 'new trekkers' into the district in the 1950s added new local pressures to conform to the racialistic norms of the south. Increasing use of motor trucks in the 1950s accelerated this influence by linking Ghanzi to neighbouring territories just at the time that apartheid policies triumphed at the South African polls. In April 1954 the Prime Minister of South Africa had moved that Bechuanaland should be transferred to the Union of South

Africa 'as soon as possible' (Horrell 1957), while in Bechuanaland itself the Ghanzi representative on the European Advisory Council urged the secession of the farming block to South West Africa.[14]

The Coloureds talk about the 1950s as 'the time the apartheid came in'. The swelling white population began to be served more regularly by *predikants* from across the border, bringing renewed sacred legitimation for segregation. They may have been influential in bringing about the excising of Coloured members from the *Gereformeerde* congregation, since it was at this time the new *Nederduitse Gereformeerde* church building was erected in the Camp, and joint services firmly instituted. In the early 1950s, the *Gereformeerde* whites with Coloured wives were, with their children, formally organised into a segregated *Gereformeerde* congregation on the farm *Rusplaas*, an event which the present *dominie* recalls sadly as a scandal. 'It was because they were kinsmen that the whites did not want to know about being together with them. . . . They would sooner have mixed with other Coloureds than with these Coloureds that were related to them.'

The observation is incisive. The greater the likelihood of assimilation, the greater the need for emphatic dissociation. The fact that Coloureds were kinsmen demanded particular public rituals of exclusion to offset the natural inclusion which flowed from the kinship bond. The ambiguous position of the Coloured kinsmen sets up ambivalent Afrikaner reaction. In public situations the ethnic definition prevails and they are excluded; in private situations the kin definition prevails and they are included.

The inconsistency is understood regretfully by the Coloureds themselves.

> Even the people from Pretoria are not as funny about colour as the Ghanzi people. The people of Ghanzi, if they want me to do a job for them, they come here and shake me by the hand and say, 'Good morning, How are you?' But the next week when I go up the Camp, or to their house, and there's a white man watching them, they don't even greet me . . . they should be ashamed. They're not straight, they'll twist and hide.

The public demonstration of separate church services was particularly resented. 'They said they could not drink out of the common communion cup with us, but after they came out of their separate church they would come and visit us and drink from our cups and sleep in our beds, lying in our blankets.'

Public rejection of Coloureds has not always been necessary. There had been a time when the community had been so intimately joined in the shameful bonds of kinship with Coloureds that no public occasions ever arose. The necessity to find wives which had prompted marriage with

Coloureds had likewise prompted marriage into the families of those who had done so. An observer in 1939 had described the 'menace' of 'inter-marrying' in Ghanzi where 'the third generation is reaching marriageable age, where further intermarriage is inevitable, owing to the fact that these youths and maidens are the only ones available within hundreds of miles and no new families are coming in' (Malherbe 1939).

The stress on the racial symbol of ethnic identity among Ghanzi Afrikaners means a concern with physical features. The startling sun-bleached blonde hair of many of the children is described proudly as 'the Ghanzi trademark'. Ideally people avoid the sun. The women's tradi-tional trekker bonnets with their projecting starched brims were designed to keep white skins white. Afrikaner shame at suntan contrasts with English attitudes, in which sun-darkened skin is a treasured status sym-bol. Nevertheless, white appearance alone will not qualify an Afrikaans-speaking person for group membership if it is known that their ancestry is part Coloured. The smelling-out of those with Coloured ancestors takes the form of what the Coloureds call *gif gooi*, throwing poison. 'If a stranger comes up and starts talking to me, somebody comes up and whispers to them, "Be careful! He is a Coloured, you know!"' It is recalled that when the white-looking children of a mixed marriage were admitted to the white school in Gobabis 'it was their very own aunties and uncles who started to *gif gooi*, saying, "Do you realise that these children are a quarter Coloured?"'

Afrikaner anxiety at being mistaken for Coloured is paralleled by Coloured anxiety at being taken for Bushmen. Coloured attitudes to Bushmen are sharply segregationist and lack the more secure paternalism of the whites.[15]

Religion provides another dimension for Afrikaner identity. The struc-ture of the Afrikaner churches is decentralised, egalitarian and par-ticipatory, based on congregational control. It is a form of organisation which so implicitly presupposes homogeneity that church membership itself has on occasions constituted sufficient and legitimate evidence of group membership, as amongst the *Gereformeerdes* in the 1930s and 1940s. Church membership and recruiting techniques are accordingly patterned on exclusive rather than inclusive lines. The careful, calculat-ing, conserving, excluding approach of the reformed churches contrasts with the more casually inclusive universalism of the newer Afrikaans Pentecostal churches, which mushroomed in South Africa in the 1950s, predictably popular with the new Afrikaner urban proletariat. The only Pentecostal farmer in Ghanzi, a newcomer, expressed the individualist rather than communal ethic in his unpopular practice of preaching to the Bushmen in the belief that their conversion was in 'the Lord's hands' rather than his own.

Yet despite Afrikaner misgivings and precautions the missionary activity of their own churches has progressed and prospered. The strict segregation of black members into separate congregations, upon which synods were able to insist in South Africa, has no future in non-racial Botswana. The traditional Afrikaner expectation that a fellow church member will be a fellow Afrikaner is no longer a sound one. In eastern Botswana, in the capital Gaborone, *Nederduitse Gereformeerde* services are held alternately in Tswana and Afrikaans, providing in effect separate services for some blacks (in Tswana) and multiracial services for whites, Coloureds and Afrikaans-speaking blacks. In isolated Ghanzi also, the confrontation with non-Afrikaner fellow religionists in common services threatens as a reality which cannot long be evaded.

The arrival in the district in 1973 of an ordained black *Nederduitse Gereformeerde dominie*, sent by a black synod in the Transvaal to evangelise the Bushmen, posed new dilemmas for Afrikaners about appropriate behaviour. The *dominie* was not simply a fellow church member, but an ordained minister, to whom particular respect was due. He was also of the black elite to whom respect was politic. The farmers cooperated with him, not only granting him access to their Bushman workers and clients, but often joining him beneath a tree at his open-air services, where they sat on chairs, listening to his message. Most offered him some kind of hospitality, shared on two occasions at their dining table. A woman asked him to come into the house to read the Bible and say prayers with her. 'It is our custom if the *dominie* visits, that he will pray with you in the house.'

The black *dominie*'s presence on the farms reminds these Afrikaners that their religion is no longer an exclusive possession, and that the racial integration of their church in Botswana is an inevitability. 'Those who are clean will be welcome', they say. 'We always envisaged one church for the clean.' But nobody has yet put this sentiment to the test among *Nederduitse Gereformeerdes*, whose *dominie* is known to have dissuaded at least one Coloured person at Xanagas from confirmation lest she present herself for worship with his congregation in Ghanzi or Gobabis. The black *dominie*, whose international experience and liberal education have given him a rare breadth of understanding and tolerance, has, at the connivance of his white clerical brothers, thus far tactfully avoided the tense confrontation of multiracial participation in church services at the Camp.

Despite its academic difficulties, church membership remains an important criterion amongst Ghanzi Afrikaners for identifying the in-group. Asked if specific marginal local people were Afrikaners, membership of the church was frequently invoked in their deliberations. 'I don't think he is really an Afrikaner but, mark you, he does go to church.' 'They do speak Afrikaans but they go to an English church.' 'Grandpa didn't mind him marrying her because she was of our church.' The congruence of Dutch Reformed church membership with Afrikanerdom was seen as altogether too complete for a Coloured man who, finding himself excluded from the latter, was determined to break with the former also. 'There are hundreds of nations in the world and each has its own belief. I think I will join the Roman Catholic church because they stick fast to their beliefs.'

V

Those who unambiguously meet all these criteria are unambivalently accepted as members of the group. Others who meet some but not all of the criteria present a classificatory puzzle both to Afrikaners and to others. They are often avoided. The way in which ambiguities are resolved, and classifications of marginal people are made, illuminates the nature of inter-ethnic relations, and of ethnicity.

The most marginal of all are the whites who have deliberately and wilfully violated group boundaries by establishing kinship relations across them, by marrying or becoming the socially acknowledged parents of a non-white. Similar relationships with white non-Afrikaners also entail a social distancing, but fail to excite the alarm and indignation which characterises kin relations with blacks.

One notorious woman bore a black baby, there are two women who have adopted black children, several men have fathered non-white children, and several have taken non-white wives. These violations of boundary-maintaining norms do not provoke equal outrage. Strongest disapproval was expressed against the woman who had the black baby, left her husband and went to live with its father, a Kgalagari. People denied knowledge of what had become of her, an eloquent expression of their rejection of her, since the likelihood that she could really have disappeared into the sparsely and intimately populated Kalahari is very low. Adoption is the least of sins, perhaps because it lacks a sexual element. Paternity is the commonest deviance.

The constraints against the total outcasting of such deviants are real. These are all Afrikaners born and bred, sons, daughters, brothers, nephews, neighbours. The weight of conditioned intimacy and acceptance is not easily or lightly laid aside as it might be in a more anonymous, less tightly knit community. Their decisive reclassification as outsiders, non-Afrikaners, is not easily accomplished, although there is no corollary of incorporation of their spouses or children. Deviants remain within the group, physically, by descent, and by social roles as traders, employees, debtors. But they are also outside it, by their deliberate choice to violate the enclosing norms. They have stepped over the boundary.

The ambiguities of their ethnic identity in an ethnically ordered world entail uncertainties in social interaction. The tendency to avoid them is as much an opting out of this uncertainty as a continued expression of social disapproval. Total avoidance is impossible.

No parallel uncertainties mark the Afrikaners' relationships with non-Afrikaner whites who have Coloured wives and children. Morality is group specific. The prevailing lack of intimacy between Afrikaners and non-Afrikaners precludes the problem of intimacy with these spouses and children. They continue to exchange labour, land, cattle, commodities and greetings with them. Socially the Coloured kin of these non-Afrikaners do not exist. In this denial Afrikaners are implicitly challenging white husbands to dare to insinuate their wives into social confrontations. One such wife, now a widow, the half-white daughter of a Bushman mother, explains,

> The whites say we cannot mix with them. The wife cannot come into the house with the white people. She sits in the car and waits for her husband. She is frightened to go in amongst the white people. . . . My children went wherever their father went. They looked like whites, they went with him to any place.

The treatment of children of these unions is crucially determined by the degree to which the white parent dominates their upbringing, and their resulting acculturation. Children actively brought up by their Bushman or Nama mothers may grow up to see themselves, and to be seen as, Bushmen or Nama. If their Afrikaner fathers take an active part in their nurture they may have much less certainty in their identity.

> My mother was a Hotnot [Nama], but I know no Hotnot because my father took me when he left her, and gave me to a Bushman wife who brought me up. My father always had a Coloured lady friend. She was a regular [*rêrige*] Coloured, not a tip top [*piekte*] Coloured like me. . . . A regular Coloured takes and marries another Coloured, and their children are regular Coloureds too. Now if a white man gads about [*rondloop*] and has a black woman, that child is a tip top Coloured like me. . . . My father's relatives receive us nicely if there are not other boers present, but if there are boers there they won't receive us. They become ashamed. I get coffee or tea, something to eat, in the kitchen not in the house. They are big [*groot-mense*], important people, white people. They don't want to sit with a coloured man. They are Afrikaners. . . . But my father, he goes inside and sits with them and talks and eats because he is a white man.

Some children, physically marginal, pass successfully into white communities, but not in Ghanzi. 'His children are taken for white in Windhoek. They have married white. You can say they are white.' Others pass successfully into black society, without suffering local black ostracism. The daughter of a white father and a Barolong mother said,

> I think it would be better if black married black and white married white. My father could not even speak good Setswana. I went to school with Coloureds in Xanagas when I was young. Then I went to Gaborone Secondary School and learned to speak like a black. Some of my brothers pass for white. Good luck to them.

White paternity of black children is most often an unplanned and unwanted social role. The deliberate creation of kinship ties with black children by adoption is a very different act. An Afrikaner woman who defied convention in adopting a black baby ('At the time I did not think she would live') finds her child, though not herself, firmly excluded from houses to which she had always been welcomed. She accepts the exclusion philosophically. 'I made my bed. I'm not asking anybody to lie on it with me.' Local Afrikaners explain:

> *Now* it goes all right, but what happens when that black child starts courting? And when her intended comes to the house to meet the parents? I don't say blacks are not good, he's just as much a person as the white man. But the Lord made differences. How come then we should choose to mix? No, I do not believe in it. There's lots of little white children they could adopt.

> She has got a lot of difficulty. The black baby is not welcome. That's what everybody around here has told her. She can't go anywhere with that child and she can't leave the child alone. So she's tied to the house with the child. My husband says the child must not come into this house. But my little daughter she always plays with her, one day here, one day there. But my husband says when she gets bigger he's not having it. It's the way people around here have been brought up; their place is outside, our place is inside.

> On New Year's Eve she took the baby with her to Jannie's, and Jannie was very put out. He did not talk to her all evening; a couple of days later Jannie came and told her, 'You're all welcome, but not the black baby.'

The black child's adoptive mother has a social life which is increasingly oriented to the Camp where expatriate European and American technical experts socialise with black officials and their families in a self-consciously integrative style.

74

What is ambiguous and marginal is best avoided. But where boundaries are clearly established, social relationships also can be established. Afrikaner identity is not simply a consequence of drawing a boundary, but of the social relationships established across that boundary. It is through their social relationships with non-Afrikaners that the group's sense of identity acquires content as well as form. Individual behaviour and attitudes are constrained by collective definitions of what, in each instance, is appropriate. Ghanzi Afrikaners are the people who patronise, employ and occasionaly sleep with Bushmen; who defer to the politically powerful, whether Tswana or British; who ignore alien Europeans; trade cattle with Herero, Barolong, Batawana and Kgalagari; but visit, marry, and are publicly intimate only with Afrikaners.

Appropriate behaviour is modified by changing circumstances. The political independence of Botswana constitutes a change in circumstance which has entailed modifications in social relationships not only with the now powerful Tswana, but, through governmental intervention, with the Bushmen as well. In the next three chapters we examine in some detail the effect of these changes in boer relations with Bushmen, as fellow Calvinists and as labourers, and in boer relations with blacks, as neighbouring pastoralists and as political masters.

Extract from transcript of tape recording, Ghanzi, 1973

Speaker: White Afrikaans man, aged 80 (and his wife, aged 68)
   Occupation: farmer
   Married, Coloured wife, adult children
   Place of birth: South Africa
   Citizenship: Motswana
   Land owned: 2000 morgen

Husband: We came into this country in 1914 from Molopo, Upington, that
   region, Zwart Modder. I was a little boy when we came. My father thought
   there would be peace in Bechuanaland for a few years. We stayed a long
   while in Lehututu. I worked for the only two whites there, traders,
   Englishmen. I also worked in Mochudi, in a shop. I was starving. I stayed
   with my sister who married the trader. In 1923 my father moved to
   Ghanzi. At first he stayed with other farmers on their land, but later we
   bought our own farm. The farms that had been abandoned by the earliest
   Transvaal settlers were sold up by the Bechuanaland government. When
   those early settlers left their farms before the thirty years was up they lost
   all claim to them. We did not pay much. It was so cheap we paid it off very
   quickly. There were only five families here when he came, but some of
   them had lots of children.

I married in 1932 in Gobabis. There was no *predikant* or Magistrate in Ghanzi then, Ghanzi had only an Under-Magistrate. I met my wife in Lehututu. She came from Rietfontein, from a farm near the *dorp*. Rietfontein is a Coloured place, near Reheboth which is a *Baster* place. Rietfontein was a missionary place, Lutheran mission. We were all together in those days, Coloureds, *Basters*, even a few European farmers.

We also stayed at Caledonia, and in Molopo on the Nossop River. There I dug wells for Coloured farmers. I worked with one old man. . . . I was the man at the bottom of the well, seventy foot down and the old man was at the top. He was too weak to pull me out with a chain so I had to make steps up and down. That was in the dry bed of the Nossop River. Those were difficult days.

My father died when he was eighty-four, on his farm. That is where he is buried. Other people have now sold that farm and the kaffirs have bought it, Damaras. When my father died the farm was divided in two. My brother farmed his half and I farmed my half. We sons had already carried on the farming when the old people got old. We also bought a second farm which we divided, which is this farm we are on today.

Wife: I had eight children. I brought them up alone, no doctors. My mother helped with the confinements. She lived here on this farm and we lived twenty miles away. They fetched my mother when the labour started. I had thirteen births, but five died. When we first came there was very bad malaria and lots of mosquitoes, and no doctor to help. Mosquitoes! You couldn't sleep. But my mother had a nature doctor book. I know the recipes off by heart I've used them so much. There was an old black man that I doctored. A lion had mauled him. The lions in those days used to come right up to the house. I doctored him just with clay, and within a month he was cured – and a lion bite is very dangerous. He was already walking when the doctor came by.

When my children come here now they say, 'Mamie, we are scared to come where there are no doctors.' I say they must remember one thing: children don't live through doctors but through the Lord. I tell them I brought up eight children without a doctor and they survived. But if they come here and one of their children gets just a little ill they get so restless.

Once my eldest daughter came and her child was a bit sick, probably with the change in water, and as soon as she arrived I gave her *Lewenessens*. She went to the Camp and came back and said that the sister at the Camp said that *Lewenessens* is no good for children with runny tummies. I said, 'Look here, I brought up eight children without a doctor. *Lewenessens* is the best medicine you can get for the stomach, anything in the stomach.' My experience told me that. Yes, if the child's stomach was worse you could have said that I made a mistake, but the child was better. Now all right! *Lewenessens* works out the trouble before it binds you. It

76

works out the trouble first. When I say that the medicine is good, then it is good. I know that medicine. I have tried it with my own experience.

Husband: She's nearly a doctor. She doctors everyone around here, even the Bushmen. I don't keep any Bushmen, I keep Batswana because I know their language. My wife talks Bushman and she has them to work for her, about four, and their wives are here also.

Wife: You have to do all your own housework here. I can't get along with Bushmen in the house. They're all right for jobs outside the house. I've only got two at the moment, I've just let a lot go [*sommer net 'n klomp los laat*]. There are Bushmen on the farm who don't work. They come and visit and stay on, and they don't want to work.

Husband: Our children all received their education on the farm. They had their own teachers, first a Hollander, then a German woman, then somebody else. The teacher had a room in the house. One of them had heart trouble.

The children are all well educated. Children of the church. They were all baptised and confirmed, and now they are all gone to South West and we are alone. They could do no other. Here is no life, in Ghanzi. There's no work in Ghanzi, they can't sit on the farm alone, as we have done. They can't stand it.

Our sons do very well for themselves, they get a lot of money. Two of our sons work on the mines at Tsumeb, and some of our sons-in-law also. They work for themselves. They'll only come here to supervise the selling of the farm or something like that. When they get the telegram saying that we're dead lots of them will come.

I have made a will. Half of the cattle are hers [his wife's], half are mine. We married in community of property. There are only a few cattle left now. For four years there has been a drought. If I am taken away everything goes to my wife. Each dry year I lose seventy or eighty cattle in the drought. If she's taken away then the manager of the Standard Bank in South West will take over and give each child an equal share. I want to go to South West to die close to my children. There would not be time when I am dying to call them to Ghanzi. A person must die with his children, not alone.

I go to church wherever I can, to hear the Lord's Word. If I'm in Ngamiland I go with the blacks in their church because I can understand their language quite as well as my own. I even go to the German church and the Roman church. They're not really so different. They do have some different beliefs but you can hear the Lord's Word in all of them. What do you think the Lord is going to do up there [he points upwards] when the Bushmen and the blacks and the whites are all up there together? Do you think He is going to have separate churches? It's too difficult a question for me to answer, I'm leaving it to the Lord, but I do have some sympathy for

77

the people who don't want to go to church with the Bushmen. There is such a thing as race and class. These Afrikaners have got apartheid in them. They can't live together. I ask myself what's the future for them in a *Tswana* country? I'm leaving. I'm going to a white man's territory.

6

Boers and Bushmen: dependence, interdependence and Independence

I

Boer relationships with Bushmen have been shaped by at least two sets of pressures, economic and political. While the more decisive role of the former cannot be denied, the latter should not be overlooked. It was administrative decision that first granted the boers pastoral rights and eventual freehold over Bushman territory, officially described with typical colonial disregard as 'vacant land',[1] because those who lived there were too unsophisticated even to lay claim to it.[2] Fuller, who led the first party of trekkers to Ghanzi in February 1894, had reported that

> the Masarwa Bushmen . . . appear to be very well disposed towards white people, in fact we have been followed by about thirty or forty of them since we have entered the country and they do not seem inclined to leave us now that we have encamped. I believe the principal reason for them wishing to be near us is that they might be protected from Segkome's people who they accuse of taking their women and children, the skins, feathers etc. that they hunt for and often killing men in addition. It is said that parties of Lake people come down occasionally purposely to get slaves etc. from amongst the Bushmen.[3]

The Afrikaners did not then come, as may be supposed, as the vanguard of a foreign invasion to shatter the idyllic peace of the Bushmen's stone-age society. They came as yet another cattle-keeping people into a situation of rivalry for the land. The Bushmen, scattered and decentralised, comprising several language groups which were themselves subdivided into small bands, lacked entirely the resources, had they the will, to present a united front against this further violation of their territory. Passarge (1907:114–20) suggests that their decentralisation was a consequence of Batawana conquest, and argues that on the Ghanzi ridge alone,

Fig. 13. Young stock on a farm on the limestone ridge. An early hewn log trough lies in the foreground

where water supplies were dependable, the Aukwe and Aikwe Bushmen had begun in the early nineteenth century to develop something approaching a centralised political structure.

Passarge records several meetings with groups of over one hundred Bushmen. On one occasion near Kwebe there were one hundred males, suggesting, with women and children, a band of three to four hundred (Passarge 1907:80, 114–20). His plausible thesis has not, however, been taken seriously by subsequent writers who have stressed the ecological necessity for the decentralised pattern they have observed.

The widespread boer adoption of local Bushman place names to identify their early farms (Ghanzies, Kgoutsa, Nughae, Naitsho, Kgoutsiri), is evidence, if any were needed, that the territory was already appropriated and minutely mapped; evidence too of the strength of the Bushman presence in Ghanzi and the Afrikaner inclination to adopt this Bushman geography rather than impose their own set of reference points.

It was administrative indifference that ignored Afrikaner pleas over the next decades 'that the Bushmen be placed in a location or given a strictly defined place to live in, for being in such a wild state they are very little use as servants'.[4] Economic forces over the next fifty years, unchecked by administrative intervention, slowly accelerated Bushman dependence on settler resources of food and water, until, in the 1970s, motivated by a curious mix of antipathy towards Afrikaners and guilt towards Bushmen, the administration finally intervened with a series of proposals to 'develop' and 'integrate' the Bushmen into contemporary Tswana society,[5] deploring the 'voluntary slavery' to which they had been reduced on the Ghanzi cattle ranches (Russell 1976).

There is historical precedent for the use of the emotive term 'slavery' to describe the clientship of Bushmen to cattle-keeping patrons. The colonial British administration had reacted in identical terms upon encountering the peculiarly underprivileged position of Bushmen and Kgalagari in the Tswana social structure in the late nineteenth and early twentieth centuries. They wrote of 'actual slavery . . . some of it of the worst and most abject kind'.[6] Yet they failed to react with the righteous indignation we might expect, cautioning against 'sudden emancipation' which would 'embarrass the slaves as well as their masters'.[7]

The institution of clientship persisted for the next forty years, so unaffected by the 'civilising influences of magistrates and missionaries' which, it had been postulated in 1887, would bring about gradual change, that the Protectorate administration was moved to action. A one-man commission of enquiry was appointed to enquire into

> the conditions under which the Masarwa are employed by the Bamangwato tribe; the nature, extent and system of their remuneration, if any; the extent to which they are free to engage in any occupations or transfer their services from one employer to the next, or move from one place to another, and able to exercise such freedom; their general conditions of life including their status in regards to the rights of person and property and the circumstances which have led to the present subject position of these people.
>
> (Tagart 1931)

The strands of alarm, concern and sympathetic insight which confused the official evaluation of clientship were drawn together in Tagart's report of 1931. He found that the Bushman clients of the Bamangwato patrons had considerable freedom to come and go as they pleased. They had an easy life which he saw as 'carefree'. They could marry and work for whom they pleased. It was 'unprogressive' and 'inconsistent with the declared policy of His Majesty's Government', but emancipation and reform needed to be permissive rather than compulsory. Although Tagart was convinced that the absence of the opportunity for cash wage labour was 'the most potent factor perpetuating the servile condition of the Masarwa', he admitted that 'the feeling amongst many of the Masarwa interviewed seemed to be lukewarm on the issue'.

The defensive report of the London Missionary Society which was published a year later argued that to describe Bushman clientship to Bamangwato patrons as 'slavery' was a misnomer.[8] Economically the Bushmen were indispensable to the Bamangwato. It was the Bushmen who had 'clung to the cattle posts of the Bechuana for preservation'. Tshekedi Khama, who had already given evidence to Tagart that his Bushmen cost him £1000 a year, contributed substantially to the London Missionary Society report, explaining how and why 'the Masarwa came to be looked upon as the people of the Bamangwato'. The report argued that the idea of weekly wages and the Western conception of work, which had provided the grounds from which the accusations of slavery had sprung, were alien to both Bushmen and Bamangwato.

The Affirmation of the Abolition of Slavery (15 of 1936) was duly proclaimed on 11 March 1936, and all District Commissioners were obliged to read the proclamation aloud in all *kgotlas*, affirming that 'the legal status of slavery does not exist, and that slavery in any form whatsoever is unlawful'. Perhaps the official view is best summed up by the District Commissioner in Serowe, who wrote:

> I think the most important accomplishment of the past year has been the announcement to thousands of Masarwa by an official that they are free . . . On the whole I think the position of the Masarwa as observed by me is fairly satisfactory . . . It is true that they do not obtain much in the way of payment for their services, but the work is not difficult and they are quite contented . . . I do not think we should try to revolutionise their evolution. Present conditions are favourable for the Masarwa to improve themselves . . . The time will arrive when they will not be willing to work for almost nothing and their masters will have the choice of paying them or losing their services.[9]

Clientship has been a central feature of inter-ethnic relations in Botswana for at least two centuries and probably much longer. It is an institution which the recent and partial introduction of wage labour is only now beginning to undermine. Something of the intricacy of the pattern of dependency is conveyed by the Resident Commissioner for Ngamiland in 1906:

> They, the subservient people of the Makoba and Botletle, are subordinate in the same sense as the BaKalahari are subordinate to the BaMangwato, the BaKwena, the BaNgwaketsi and the BaKhatle; and as the Masarwa are subordinate to the BaKalahari and as the Masarwa are subordinate to the Makoba themselves . . . as far as I can see the essential elements of slavery are all wanting.[10]

Schapera (1930:233; 1938:30–1) provides more recent and more authoritative confirmation of the pattern of ranked ethnic groups within the Tswana tribal structure. The subservience of the Bushmen to the Kgalagari as observed in the 1960s has been characterised by Kuper and Silberbauer (1966) as serfdom: 'Bushmen are free to marry, raise families and enjoy their traditional social life to a degree which forbids the description of their condition as slavery' (A. Kuper 1970:44–8).

II

In 1900 the Ghanzi Bushmen, unlike those whose territory lay on the eastern periphery of the Kalahari, had never known full clientship. They were, in the parlance of the day, 'wild Bushmen', meaning that they had not been subjected to the changes which clientship brings. From the beginning the relationship between boer and Bushman had been an uneasy symbiosis. Although the boers had trespassed on the Bushmen's traditional hunting and gathering territory, that territory was extensive, and the boers very few in number. In the Bushman view they presented an alternative to Batawana overlordship, a possibly more benign alternative, since these particular trekkers had no tradition of slave owning, a practice which had been the prerogative of the richer, more settled farmers. Although Afrikaners came to Ghanzi familiar with the idea of the services of blacks for many menial tasks, it is significant that they brought no servants with them, although they acquired the services of local Bushmen in domestic and farm labour.

Like the Tswana they used the Bushmen as trackers and stalkers of game, sharing the meat but not the trophies, in which there was an established if erratic trade. As hunters they were to some extent rivals, a rivalry which they still feel and express.[11] But game was plentiful, and despite occasional mutual complaints about the rate at which the other was denuding the veld, as hunters they could and did coexist. The berries and fruits, roots and nuts which the Bushmen gathered became sufficiently incorporated into Afrikaner diet to receive Afrikaans names, but they never replaced the Afrikaner staples of maize, pumpkin and meat.

As pastoralists the boers found their interests opposed to those of the hunting Bushmen. Not only did hungry hunters yield to the temptation of easy meat from calf or ox, but they burned off the boers' grazing to attract game to the open plains of new green grass.[12] The cattle were both troubled and made wild by the thousands of game, especially wildebeest, thus lured onto the unfenced land. Initially no boer entrusted his herds to Bushmen. This work was reserved for farmers' sons. Boer and Bushmen also squabbled over *tsamma* melons, a Bushman staple, which the boers used chiefly as cattle feed.

Yet the surface water continued to draw boer and Bushman together, as well as the game which congregated to drink from it. As over the next thirty years the water table steadily declined, boer skill at sinking wells put them at a decisive economic advantage over the Bushmen for the first time. When in the early 1950s the further decline in water levels necessitated the more complex technology and capitalisation of borehole and pump, Bushman dependence was further accelerated.

Any Bushman power relative to the boers rested on the extent of boer dependence on their labour. Initially the demand for labour was very low. In the 1930s, however, the practice of creaming produced the first labour-intensive cattle task the Afrikaners had known. Cows which had calved had to be brought in, kraaled and milked. For the first time Bushmen were widely drawn into the boer economy, receiving a daily share of milk, and a weekly share of the imported boer foods for which they had acquired a taste; maize meal, tea, coffee and sugar. They were also given clothes. 'We clothed the Bushmen', Afrikaners proudly say. 'Before we came they were naked.' 'You could say that almost anything they needed, you could pay it to them.'

At first the Bushmen neither needed, nor asked for, money, which was as well since the boers would have been unable to provide it. Creaming was undertaken only by those poorer settlers who had no other source of cash, not even cattle to sell. The whole creaming venture was an endeavour by the poorest Afrikaners to acquire cash.

Even amongst creamers the demand for labour was spasmodic, seasonal, and seldom intensive. Indeed no other demand would have easily been met. The Bushman herders were not formally or forcefully tied to the cattle owner.[13] The attractions of summer fruit and seasonal game drew Bushmen away for months at a time. They returned only after the pans had baked to a hard white crust, and the long grass withered to blonde straws, and their sip wells dried beyond use.

The spasmodic gifts of food from boer to Bushmen slowly became institutionalised as 'rations', yet the recipient retained a partial nomadism, one foot in the pastoralist's world, one foot in his own. The pastoralists, convinced that all proper men, whether socially inferior or not, should own cattle, sometimes rewarded clients of long standing with an ox or a calf, to enable the hunter to found a modest herd and enter the superior world of the pastoralist. Invariably the hunter ate the gift. 'They're not a nation that like to keep anything. They do not like the responsibility of looking after things. You've never seen a rich Bushman.' As long as the Bushmen could retain a foothold in both worlds, and as long as the two worlds remained compatible, the immediate affluence of hunting and foraging was preferred to the deferred and time-bound rewards of pastoralism (Sahlins 1974).

Until the 1940s most of the Afrikaners remained on the margins of the cash economy. Their hostility to wage labour lay not so much in an aversion to labour as in aversion to the acceptance of a wage, the consequences of which they had seen, and did not like. Cattle lending was popular amongst them because it lacked the demeaning wage element. Instead of dividing the community it cemented it more firmly together. The exchanges between client and patron established similar bonds of mutual dependence, and a kind of relationship very different from the calculating separation of employer and employee. By the 1940s cash was intruding into the Kalahari. Lorries were carrying Bushmen into the outside world of consumers. Stores at Ghanzi began to sell for cash rather than to trade in exchanges (chiefly pelts). Bushmen who as early as 1927 had, like their patrons, been trading *maklossie* and jackal furs at Kgoutsa, discovered that increasing labour reduced their opportunities for hunting. The cash element in the client–patron relationship began to assume a greater importance.

The decade of decisive transformation was the 1960s. The sale of farms and their fencing suddenly made private the undemarcated veld: 'our land' became 'my land' to the successful purchaser. The intended pressure towards commercial ranching awoke a new awareness of costs, margins of profit and labour efficiency. The Bushmen found their world divided and their movements increasingly hampered by *die draad*, the transforming fencing wire. Some of the new freehold ranchers had no time for what they saw as the casual laxity of Bushman clients, and dispensed entirely with their labour, introducing in their stead African labourers housed in farm compounds and clad in issue blue boiler suits. The Bushmen's traditional generosity in a world of reciprocal giving provided additional grounds for their redundancy: 'When we gave them rations for themselves everybody came and ate.' 'They did not keep themselves tidy; they gave their uniforms to their friends.' The goal of efficient, well-fed workers is not easily attained without the appropriate selfishness of the worker.

The old uneasy truce between hunter and pastoralist patron is being replaced by the classical conflict between employer and worker. The two idioms coexist confusingly. Some Bushmen continue as clients to receive small cash wages, substantial food rations[14] and a host of hidden favours: the certainty of a welcome beside the water tank for themselves and their dependents, the loan of transport animals, the opportunity to share gun hunting, casual paid employment opportunities for kinsmen, including sought-after domestic service for girls with its perquisites in food, clothing and travelling. Where emphasis is on clientship rather than wage labour, the corollaries are personal knowledge of the clients, rather than the welfare of the worker. There is an acceptance of idiosyncrasies rather than a demand for regularity and uniformity. The dominant motif is

Fig. 14. A seventy-two-year-old widow farming alone accompanies her workers daily to the veld to light a fire and cook food in the traditional iron pot. 'Some people expect men to work on an empty stomach.'

paternalism, with its implications of both benign concern and sharp status difference. In 1973 a farmer's wife drove forty miles in her truck to leave a message for the doctor that a Bushman (not one of 'hers') had been seriously injured in a fight. When a Bushman worker died ('He was an old man, he had been with me a long time'), the farmer took the body and the mourners on the back of his truck to the burial place on his farm, where he read a short passage from the Bible to them, and said a short prayer. 'And then I left them because they have their own ways in these matters but I felt that I must commend him to the Lord.'

The sharp status difference creates the framework within which intimacy is tolerable (van den Berghe 1972), since it threatens neither the integrity of the group nor the status of the participating individuals as group members. The intimacy comes from prolonged acquaintance, the outcome of a small, stable population sharing the same space. The anonymous collective, 'Bushmen', so present in the minds of visiting outsiders like ourselves, comes into sharp focus in conversation with Afrikaners as a number of carefully delineated individuals, whose names, parents, birthplaces, biographies, quirks and foibles are known. If you say to a group of Afrikaners, 'A Bushman told me,' they will interrupt to ask, 'Which Bushman?', and will then amongst themselves piece together, on

86

the basis of your poorly observed information ('Did he wear a red woollen hat? Was he tattoed between the eyebrows? Was he with his yellow skinned wife?') who your informant was. 'That must have been Tshali from Buitsavango. I wonder what he was doing on your side.'

Whereas the client has a foot in both worlds, the worker must stand exclusively in the new world. A step towards the old world, a sudden absence, means dismissal. Wages owed will be paid, but the boiler suit must be returned for the use of the successor.

The Bushman's status, whether client or worker, corresponds to the level of modernisation achieved by his patron or employer. The new commercial ranchers are employers. The world of the farm has begun to diverge radically from that of the veld. The change is not so much physical, though the fences have certainly altered the ecology, inhibiting game and encouraging erosion of the smaller overstocked farm. The change is social. It is most profound at the level of values and nowhere is this more clearly expressed than in labour relations.

Ironically, clientship persists even on those farms where efficient black labour has replaced Bushman clientship, for the black employees frequently bring their own clients with them, to look after their herds and share in their water. Here too a cash element has intruded. One such Bushman client in 1973 was in receipt of one rand a month from his Kgalagari patron employed by a white farming company. Six adult Bushmen were sharing the Kgalagari's patronage, a state of affairs which the farm manager accepted with a sigh as inevitable, though on other farms measures were being taken to evict the herds, if not the clients.

As workers, Bushmen are in direct competition from other ethnic groups whose cattle-keeping background makes them an attractive alternative as employees. The cessation of creaming has reduced the overall local demand for labour. New labour tasks – fencing, pumping, insemination and innoculation – demand a sophistication which some farmers feel is more easily found in black rather than Bushman workers. The demand for Bushman labour has never been lower. The economic dispensability of many local Bushmen to the ranchers is beyond doubt. A government survey in 1975 estimated that of 4000 Bushmen living on the farms, 675 were employed by farmers, 2050 were 'the immediate family of these employees' and 1275 were 'unwanted squatters . . . generally part of the kinship group of farm employees'.[15] Of the five dependents to each employee, two or three are likely to be adult.

The indispensability of the farmers to the Bushmen is reflected in government findings on Bushman reaction to their proposal to create Bushman settlement farms in Ghanzi, to free Bushmen from the necessity of finding employment with farmers. Of the 1016 Bushmen interviewed (presumably all heads of households) 56 per cent expressed a wish to continue in employment on the farms, either permanently or occasionally, while 44 per cent expressed 'an intense desire to stay permanently at . . . a settlement of their own'. Options would seem to have been strongly influenced by experienced employment opportunities. Assuming that all 'unwanted squatters' welcomed the government's proposals, only some 20 per cent of employed Bushmen expressed a desire to quit farm employment.[16]

The transformation of patron–client relations to those of employer–worker is accelerated by administrative pressure. A new labour officer was appointed to Ghanzi in 1974. Exploratory memoranda on labour conditions in Ghanzi had deplored conditions, and raised the possibility of minimum wages, paid leave, maternity leave and toilet facilities (Ghanzi Labour Inspection Report, November 1971). The parallels with the situation in the 1930s are manifold. Neither British nor Botswana officialdom can be seen as having any but the best intentions for the Bushmen, but in both instances the idiom is the inappropriate one of the modernised world of industrial labour relations, with its limitation of mutual obligation, its contract, its specificity. The implications for the Bushmen are grave. One farmer, in order to emphasise his dilemma, gathered all the 'superfluous' Bushmen from his farm and deposited them in front of the District Commissioner's office. Others, faced with the Labour Department's intention of declaring all Bushmen on the farms to be workers, and hence due to receive wages, say that they will not be able to afford to let the Bushmen live on their farms in the future, and ask in perplexity where they will go. The rights of the Bushmen to be in Ghanzi have always been conceded by the local Afrikaners, though they have in the past fiercely contested the immigration of all others.[17]

The reduction of present relations to contract terms cannot be without loss to the Bushmen. For whatever the principle, the present practice is underemployment. The patron who feels an obligation to let his clients take milk or borrow donkeys, who gives them soap and tobacco and occasional meat, is unlikely to commit himself to such generosity in a contractual undertaking, not least because he does not share the reformers' vocabulary, and where he understands it, he resists the values implicit in it. The problem, for patrons and clients, is not one of a few people clinging to an outmoded social institution in an otherwise modern context, but of the intrusion into the lives of many in an unmodernised context, of the values of another world.

III

The frequent sexual intimacy of Afrikaner men and Bushman women is typical of the colonial situation whenever European adventurers advanced frontiers. The sexual imbalance in the newcomers' population inevitably led them into liaisons with local women. Perhaps physical and sexual adventuring go hand in hand. Although it is fashionable to depict this behaviour as racial exploitation (historical accident made the whites the adventurers in a black world), the same phenomenon has been observed amongst twentieth-century Italian immigrants to Australia, where early sexual integration with local (white) women was replaced by social withdrawal as Italian wives followed, reasserting the culture of origin. In the United Kingdom intermarriage is usually between white girls and immigrant (black) men (Allen 1971:114).

Liaisons with Bushman women were very common in the early twentieth century: 'in the old days we all did it'. It remains more typical of the older generation of men, many of whom keep Bushman concubines, some of whom have never married white wives. Most liaisons are clandestine, but not effectively so; the society is too intimate for secrets, particularly when one party feels no shame about participation. This behaviour is typically condoned by men, the subject of sly boasting between them. Bushmen regard the matter with philosophical resignation, taking care that it is their daughters but never their wives who are drawn into such relations. For many generations dominant groups – Nama, Herero, Kgalagari and Tswana – have taken Bushman women, often looking after them well, putting themselves marginally in the Bushman debt, offering families a more careful patronage because of this bond. The liaisons vary from prostitution ('he gives my daughter three rand to sleep with him when his wife is away') to marriage in full accord with Bushman norms, which, in the propertyless society, do not carry the implications of lifelong fidelity and commitment that Afrikaners expect of one another. Marriage means social paternity, the commitment to the responsibility of raising children.

From the Afrikaner viewpoint, impregnation within these liaisons constitutes a very serious breach of norms, imposing on the whole community the strain of indeterminate social obligation, threatening to transform the casual private liaison into the inescapable public bond of kinship. The whole community is threatened since the reciprocal bonds of kinship pull the whole community into the dilemma. One way of resolving the problem is the adoption of the child by a man who is not an Afrikaner, with financial settlement by the natural father in lieu of full paternal responsibility. In this way the obligation of the natural father is honourably discharged and the Afrikaner community is collectively released from kinship. But residual disapproval of the guilty man is ineradicable, despite this symbolic statement by him that the liaison was wrong; that kinship between Afrikaners and Bushmen is not possible. The alternative, frank acceptance of paternity and its implications, entails social exclusion. Bushmen kin are renounced by the renunciation of the kinship bond with the deviant. Yet total social exclusion is impossible. Close kin surreptitiously receive their deviant relations. The rest of the community suppresses the kinship link in their unavoidable confrontations with them. As traders, workers, or customers, even deviants remain a part of Ghanzi society, their green-eyed Bushman children a constant reminder of the intimacy between groups.

There was only one Afrikaner man married to a Bushman and living with her in 1973 in Ghanzi. He was living under a *machara* tree in his portable corrugated iron 'tent', with his third wife, a Nharo, his three olive-skinned daughters, and a household of Kgalagari and Bushman domestic servants, workers and dependants, who helped him with the contract fencing, dam building and other jobs at which he earned his living. His cattle were on hired grazing on an Afrikaner's farm. He described his childhood as the son of a schoolmaster become trader, in the Okavango swamps, living in a stick house. He was his father's herdsman and his work was watering the cattle which his father traded for commodities from *onderaf* (down yonder). There were nine hundred cattle and all the water had to be raised by hand from a well. His father got grazing land in Ghanzi and later acquired a farm. He was twenty-four years old when he got his first child from a Nama woman, with whom he slept under a tree, not daring to bring her into his father's house. He did not live with her. 'I'd go to her when I needed anything like washing my clothes, and when she was near me we slept together, and then she'd go back to her own people.' When he got the baby he 'told the whole lot about it . . . I did not hide it and they were angry, but what does it help to hide it away? . . . Some men were not angry because they did just as I did. They slept with Bushmen . . . in the beginning nearly everybody was a *rondloper* [literally 'one who walks about'; carrying strong connotations of promiscuity].' The weight of disapproval came from the white women. 'They still talked to me, but they held themselves superior. They did not want me to think that I was now going to get a white woman. I did not mind. I had made my mistake. I could not have both black and white, so I hold what I've got.'

His mistake was to have the child, not to sleep with the woman. It is still expected of young men that they will have sexual adventures with Bushmen much as the Victorians patronised prostitutes. The small scale of Ghanzi society deprives these exploits of their anonymity. 'Everyone knows; the Bushmen are not the sort who hide anything.' Common knowledge of deviance does not shake Afrikaner conviction in the essential propriety of the social distance from Bushmen which their norms prescribe.

The intimacy of marriage is unusual; and clandestine sexual relations,

Fig. 15. Afrikaner with common law Bushman wife and children outside his house. Ghanzi, 1973

though common, are screened by subterfuge. More visible and common are the bonds of intimacy established between pairs of peers linked in childhood as *maties* (playmates). These persist into adult life. People say, 'He has been with me all my life.' It is through the institution of *maties* that Bushmen come to know Afrikaners by their first, their intimate, names rather than by any other. The use of first names in European cultures would denote either intimacy or equality, or the superiority of the nominator over the nominated. None of these holds for Ghanzi. This anomaly confuses European outsiders: the apparent signalling of equality within apparently very unequal relationships. Thus in 1973 the visiting Magistrate, cross-questioning a Bushman witness, had the greatest difficulty in establishing the identity of the Afrikaner accused.

> *Magistrate:* Do you know this man?
> *Witness:* I do.
> *Magistrate:* Who is he?
> *Witness:* He is Kassie.
> *Magistrate:* Has he another name?
> *Witness:* I do not know.
> *Magistrate:* Is he Caspanus Gerhard Hendrik de Villiers?
> *Witness:* No. He is Kassie.

Intervention by the prosecution suggested that common sense rather than legal nicety should prevail in this as in other respects in justice in Ghanzi.[18]

The case itself was not without significance: the prosecution of a young Afrikaner for assaulting a young Bushman whom he suspected of stealing an empty plastic petrol bottle, known locally as 'the nylon' and carrying a far higher scarcity value in Ghanzi than could be imagined in the throw away, plastic-wrapped Western world. It was not the first case of assault to reach the courts, though Afrikaner breaches of law are few. Between 1970 and 1973 only nine of the 417 criminal cases heard in Ghanzi involved Afrikaners, and seven of these were for infringements of the hunting licence regulations. Fittingly the most prevalent crime amongst hunters is stealing cattle, the most prevalent amongst pastoralists is stealing game.

Afrikaner opinion on the assault case was divided and fairly open. Some said darkly that 'He'd had it coming to him for a long time' and 'If he gets away with this he can get away with anything.' Others said it was likely that the 'Bushmen are just making up a case against him.' Whether the verdict was to be guilty or not guilty, there was a general feeling that 'They want to show us that we cannot do with the Bushmen what we like.' 'They want to show us that Ghanzi gaol is also for the Afrikaners.'

In the event the government probably succeeded in both these imputed aims. The accused was found guilty and was goaled for a month (ironically to share the little Ghanzi lock-up with the Bushman whom he had assaulted, who was found guilty of theft), and there was much intense discussion among Afrikaners of the changing situation, in which the legal access of the Bushmen to the courts was not merely theoretically affirmed but practically demonstrated. The extent of the innovation is better appreciated against the traditional exclusion of the Bushmen from the normal processes of law in the Tswana villages (Schapera 1930, 1938; A. Kuper 1970).

The earlier Afrikaner institutions for the settlement of grievances between themselves and the Bushmen are reflected in the terms in which Bushmen assess Afrikaners. 'They are very good people because . . . they do not let other people hit you.' 'Mrs van den Berg is very bad tempered. She hit! She used to hit the gardener with a belt when he didn't work, and she swore at him.' Nor has access to the courts entirely eliminated the customary practice.

> I was prosecuted for hitting a Bushman, before the black Magistrate. I came home at Christmas and he was nice and drunk, and he threw a stone at me. Now then, I hit him a good hiding with my fist. I paid five rand admission of guilt. Usually I pay admission of guilt. It's now illegal to hit a Bushman without grounds, for example that he hit you first. But then you'd need good witnesses or it won't help you. The administration are strict about that.

Corporal punishment is also in the Tswana tradition, particularly for offenders with no property to be attached, where its use is contrained by public opinion in the *kgotla*. There are no parallel formal constraints on Afrikaners, though Afrikaner opinion operates informally against indiscriminate violence. 'I told him he could not carry on hitting Bushmen. The man is a sadist.' Humanitarian constraints are reinforced with utilitarian considerations. 'We who have been in Ghanzi a long time do not lose our patience with the Bushmen. When they go away you have to know that they will come back and when they do you will be glad to see them.' There is also fear of physical reprisals, especially poisoning.

IV

Afrikaner attitudes to the Bushmen in whose midst they live have been curiously affected by the Tswana rise to power in government and administration. Afrikaner response to the new paternalistic concern for the Bushmen, which the administration has adopted since Independence, is to vie with the Tswana. A fierce rivalry for the loyalty of the Bushmen exists, each group maligning the other in this respect whenever the occasion presents itself. Thus Bushman antipathy towards a Tswana official in 1971 and their satisfaction with their working conditions was officially interpreted as the consequence of 'malicious spiteful propaganda . . . lubrication for this type of slavery' (Ghanzi Labour Inspection Report, November 1971).

In summary, the relationship of the Afrikaners to the Bushmen is characterised by intimacy, familiarity and inequality. It is a relationship between highly bounded groups whose distinctiveness is in no way obscured by sexual intimacy across the boundary. The economic dependence of the Bushmen on the boers is the consequence of the gradual alienation of the Bushman land rights on the less arid limestone ridge, and the superior water technology of the whites which had enabled the boers to penetrate Bushman territory. Commercialisation of cattle-keeping is transforming this territory at a drastic rate, cutting away both the Bushmen's traditional hunting and gathering economy, and the opportunities for secure clientship. As employees the Bushmen now compete with the more experienced blacks.

Boer attitudes to Bushmen are informed by all these circumstances and consist of so many aspects that generalisation is difficult and probably misleading. How, for instance, should we characterise the attitudes towards Bushmen of an Afrikaner in Ghanzi with a Bushman mistress? Would we be content with his publicly conformist statements about racial differences, neolithic life style, unreliability as workers? Or would we need to add to this the more accepting tolerant and egalitarian statements he would be careful to make to the critical outsider, anthropologist or official? What weight should we attach to his amorous private behaviour? Would we be justified in concluding that attitudes were a fickle and unimportant datum for the understanding of a social situation? In chapter 8 we shall reconsider these questions in the context of prevailing sociological approaches to the problem of race and ethnicity.

Extract from transcript of tape recording, Ghanzi, 1973

Speaker: White Afrikaans man, aged 58
   Occupation: farmer and trader
   Married, polygamous. First wife: Coloured, 9 children. Second wife: half white half Herero, 2 children
   Place of birth: Angola
   Citizenship: Motswana
   Land owned: 12 000 morgen

There used to be about 150 Afrikaans families in Angola, where I was born, and they lived in shocking conditions. They were poor and they had no prospects. They were dispersed, not concentrated, because they made their living from transport; they could not live close together lest they cut each other's throat, competing for transport. They rode transport with oxen and wagon, from Lobito to the hinterland. They took raw rubber down to the coast and brought back salt, which was very scarce and precious, and meal and clothing. The hinterland was terribly primitive in those days. There was some sowing of seeds and some crop cultivation, but on a very small scale. But that was not what put people off, it was that as strangers they had no privileges. The Portuguese authorities wouldn't grant them citizenship. They were regarded as strangers. Now you can easily imagine that if you are not regarded as a citizen you are not a settled resident there. There are many rights that one would imagine a resident would have, like title to freehold land, that they never got. They were permitted to ride transport, and to trade and to erect some sort of little dwelling; but this style of life was unacceptable, because they were regarded as strangers.

I was nine years old when my father came to us and said, 'Look children, I don't want to make decisions for everybody, I want to hear your point of view, we must make a joint decision in accordance with everybody's wishes.' We were seven children, I was the fifth. Even I, who was only nine years old, he specially asked me, 'What do you think? Shall we go back where our nation is? Or shall we remain among strangers?' I said – even as a child I thought a person must be loyal to his nation – 'No,' I said, 'Let us go back.' You might think I simply wanted the journey, but I really did feel that, even though I was a child – and the Lord did not let me down!

The method of the administration of the Portuguese at that time was to me terrible. They had a frightening sense of superiority [*'n verskriklike lae oog*]. He thought he was the best and that there never could be another person as good as he. So whether he be black or white or coloured or whatever, there was in his eyes only one decent kind of person, and that was a Portuguese. He alone had any wisdom or understanding, and he alone had the right to govern. Now, well, that gets anybody, to know this somebody looks at you with a contemptuous eye. It was clear to me that we would never achieve any equality or community [*saamlewing*], we would never serve the same Lord – and I don't mean in church – we would never pledge the same honour to the state. Child as I was, I thought it would be very nice, though we would be very poor and have many difficulties, to go back where we would feel at home, no matter how gruelling the conditions would prove themselves.

And there were difficulties. Transport was very difficult, food was scarce. It was a long journey from Behe, in the heart of Angola, to South West.

I grew up in Rehoboth in South West. In those days General Hertzog was Prime Minister. He was a nationalist. He felt that Afrikaaners ought to stay together, and remain in southern Africa. He thought it was necessary to keep them together for the preservation of Afrikanerdom.

95

I myself did not like South West and its laws. In my eyes it was discriminating. I was now talking as an adult. When you grow up you begin to examine and criticise policies. I grew up in South West African politics. There were aspects that were very nice to me, but there were aspects with which I couldn't agree. Now if you don't like a thing, you don't quarrel and start a war, you try to find somewhere else where you will be satisfied. I would not say Botswana is a better place to stay than South West Africa – never! But I will say it is better for me. I feel happier here, freer. I have here privileges I was denied in South West. For example, as a youngster I had very little schooling. I therefore was directed to an occupation that an uneducated man can follow – farming. But in South West there was no land for single men. The demands of married people were so overwhelming that single people couldn't get farms. So I decided to go, not to Botswana, just to any place where I could get a farm of my own, where I could begin. It was in my blood to farm. It was the only job I could do because I was uneducated.

In 1950 I heard that Botswana had great need of people who could bore for water. So I decided I would accept this invitation. I came on 4 December 1951, and I bored water so that the government was satisfied, and I bored water so that the farmers were satisfied! (I was paid by the government, but I also bored for private people.) I decided I wanted to farm here and the government said, 'Good, you have helped us and now we will help you. That little farm you are occupying we will measure off, and here is the price. You can buy, and pay off slowly, and it will be yours.'

Now I am not a burden on anybody, not the South West administration, not Botswana, because I have worked for the privilege of owning the land. The Botswana government have kept their promises, I am satisfied.

All my life I have been regarded as a stranger, even in South West. There I remained on the trek route [i.e. he did not settle]. If you ask me if I'll ever think of returning to South West or the Republic [South Africa] I'll say 'Never!' That is definite. I don't talk politics, I talk about myself, and how I am affected. Botswana has allowed me to live. You can't be cross with the hand that feeds you. Since the Bechuanas themselves took over from the British they've handled me just the same.

There are many of us whites who ran away from the Botswana government, who sent their children to school far away when they were still small. I can't see that was necessary. It is a fact that the children have been born here, for good or evil, this is their land. These children of mine that are born here, I want them to grow up as it is now. They must be true to the conditions as they are now.

Look, in the old days the boers were untouchable, unapproachable, just like the Portuguese, very proud. He always considered his integrity a little bit higher than anybody else's. My children can't be brought up to think so. They are citizens of the land, they are born here, they have to make a living here. Of course they are free to go where they choose, but I can't see why they shouldn't be brought up here as far as possible. They can get educated here as far as standard seven, then they go to secondary school.

One of my children is writing her jaycee [junior school leaving certificate] in Gaborone. When she's finished she must go elsewhere for more education. She can go to Washington or Windhoek, it's all the same to me as long as she gets the learning. She's got to learn to get on with all the people of this land, and she can. She can speak to anybody in their own language. We can't see into the future, but I think all young lands, they all have their growing pains. We can't see which one is going to get ahead, which one is dangerous, which safe. Botswana has developed enormously in the twenty years I've been here, and that's not to say it's due to the wonderful outstanding rule of the black man, not at all. Time itself has brought development. You can say we've been through a period of transition, it hasn't really been dependent on government, just the passing of time.

South West was very underdeveloped twenty years ago, a goat cost one and a half rand. They now have developed much further than Botswana but they had a bigger start than Botswana. I predict in ten or fifteen years' time we'll have nothing to complain of in Botswana. Actually I've got no reason to complain now. I lack nothing. My children are well mannered and well cared for at school. I am handled sympathetically by the government. I've got my farm, I've got my cattle and small stock. I'm free to slaughter them if I want to and to sell if I want to. I've got my own shop, quite a good shop too. But we have no reason to feel superior. The land develops like any other land.

Naturally you can't keep all your children with you and let them all stay on the farm, but as they grow up other provision is made for them. Botswana must look after its citizens. It's enough that I have paid school fees for them when they were small. Now they must see what they can do with them.

I want them to grow up faithful to the circumstances as they are today. There is no longer the lord and the lackey [*die grootbaas en die kneg*]. We are all people.

A person can hardly believe that I, a boer right out of South West, can be happy here. But I am, I am not harassed, not deprived of my rights. Now things have changed. It's very comfortable here if you are willing to act in the right way, if you are willing to accept little things that are quite irrelevant to your own standards. It is also one of the safest places. The worst that can happen to me here can also happen to the Prime Minister of the Republic of South Africa – I can die.

In the summer it's a very pretty land. In the rain I plough and get enough food out of the land to feed myself and my family and my servants. There are at least fifty people that eat out of my hand, many servants, Bushman, Kgalagari, Batswanas and their families. I pay them money and food. I pay them money because I grew up as a labourer and it was terribly difficult to work and not to receive money at the end of it. That was a lesson for my life. If a person works for me he must not be hungry and he must get money. The people around here used to be so mean that they paid servants two or three rand a month. I pay them twelve rand and a month's leave a year and if they give me good service I give them bonuses and *bonselas*. There are some Bushman families that live permanently on the farm, but there are other migrant workers [*los werkers*] who work on a particular job and then they leave. They may come back ten times. But if he's a *dronklap* [drunkard] or a *skelm* [rogue], I call him on the second day and say, 'Boy, here's your money. Go, don't come back.'

Heavens! If a person lives in Botswana and can't get labourers the fault is definitely with him. Botswana is a land of labourers. But a person must behave with humanity, and pay for the services, then you'll get crowds! Every day there are people looking for work at my place.

7

Sharing religion: attitudes to the conversion of the Bushmen to Christianity

I

In 1973 the small *Gereformeerde* congregation of twenty-five members at D'Kar was formally dissolved. Three pastors representing the *Gereformeerde* synod presided over the dissolution. They had travelled by car from Mariental in Namibia to the Botswana border, and there a truck driven by one of the congregation had met them to bring them the last three hundred kilometres to the church farm at D'Kar. In the church farmhouse they met with the men of the congregation. There were only eight of them. Yet it was not the smallness of number which prompted the dissolution. There had been fewer than twenty-one families when the congregation had been established in 1948 and no anticipation then of any startling increase in numbers.[1] 'The *Gereformeerde* do not go by strength of numbers but by strength of faith', the *dominie* said. 'In this we are unlike our sister church the *Nederduitse Gereformeerde*.'

The cause for dissolution was more significant: a directive from the Botswana government that the existence of the white Afrikaner congregation alongside a mission to the Bushmen by the self-same denomination was contrary to the government policy of non-racialism, and that the white congregation should in future amalgamate with the Bushman mission congregation.

In this chapter we consider the D'Kar congregation's response to the establishment of the mission and explore their attitudes to attempts at converting the Bushmen to Christianity. We suggest that they exemplify the dilemmas, conflicts and tensions which characterise confrontations between settlers and missionaries; the isolation of the Kalahari context serves to throw into peculiarly sharp relief the inherent problems for all settlers of the universalist impulse of Christianity.

Christianity, like Islam and Buddhism, is a universal religion in the sense that its membership is potentially open to everybody.[2] The proselytising injunction was enshrined and legitimated early in its sacred text (Matthew 28:19–20). The impulse to act upon it has waxed and waned, superficially it would seem in proportion to the imperialist expansionist inclinations of its bearers, though whether this is to be construed as cause or consequence is debatable. Clearly, colonies represented an opportunity which the religiously fervid could seize, but on occasion missions preceded colonial powers, and frequently acted for them in negotiation and administration (Mehl 1970:163–88). The impulse to proselytise and the impulse to colonise are bedfellows; indigenous peoples had frequent difficulty in distinguishing them. Certainly in the long run the kinds of changes initiated by missionaries went far towards creating a demand for the commodities which irrevocably brought the post-colonial territories into permanent interdependence with, if not dependence on, the colonising powers from which the missionaries originally came.

Proselytising is a curious activity. It is the deliberate and self-conscious attempt to change the world view of people, to substitute for an exisiting world view a new sacred cosmos (Berger 1969:26), and endow that new world view with such legitimacy that it seems uniquely realistic (Geertz 1966). The task is formidable and the conspicuous lack of success of many missionaries in many places is hardly surprising. Equally understandable are the continuing missionary doubts as to the validity of the religious experience of the converted.[3] Intuitively the missionaries were grappling with the problem which received explicit sociological articulation in the 1960s: how much else besides theology, besides what Berger so aptly characterises as sacred cosmos, must be changed if the new world view is to receive that daily social affirmation without which it is unlikely to be maintained? The problem is one of the relative autonomy of the 'parts' of the social fabric. Bellah, in his evolutionary approach to religion, has suggested that autonomy is a central criterion of evolution; the more highly evolved religion is precisely the one which can be transferred, adopted, without repercussion in or implication for other areas of social life. He contrasts the socially constraining permeation of the medieval Christianity in the European social fabric with the more evolved free-wheeling private nature of many contemporary American beliefs about their relationships with the ultimate conditions of their existence (Bellah 1964:263).

The struggle of contemporary Christian missionary effort to free itself of specific cultural constraints may be interpreted as evolutionary advance, in Bellah's terms, in so far as it reduces the scope the implications of the religious to a narrow concern with particular solutions to philosophical problems of meaning, salvation or the ultimate. It might be argued that it is the very process of universalism that pares down the religious function, and thus promotes its evolution.

In these terms, the Christianity of the nineteenth-century Protestant missionaries must be seen as less evolved. The establishment of Christian villages in India and Christian reserves in Africa show that a change of world view was seen to carry very specific social consequences.[4] Special arrangements had to be made to enable converts to maintain their new ideology whose ethic frequently insisted *inter alia* on entry into paid wage labour, in the classic Protestant mode described by Weber, Tawney, Thompson and others. Universalism also carried very specific social consequences for its bearers, the Christians, but not for all of them equally.

II

The universalist nature of Christianity is a remote consideration for most Christians, since their local organisation into congregations is usually in accordance with local social distinctions. The denominations are themselves as much a form of social as doctrinal differentiation (Niebuhr 1964). Neighbourhood location has also ensured homogeneity, and where this has not been so, as in parish churches serving entire villages, there was in the past careful congregational reinforcement of local social distinctions, for example in the allocation of family pews. In contemporary times people with cars travel the distance necessary to ensure their worship with agreeable others – to the distress of church authorities.[5]

Thus in Britain the Christian experience is of the relatively homogeneous congregation; their confrontation with universalism is usually restricted to the singing of sentimental songs about benighted men on 'Afric's golden sand' (Heber 1933). It is a shock when, in fulfilment of their song's expressed wishes, the benighted are delivered from error's chain and arrive from Afric's golden sand, via Jamaica, on their church steps, expecting a brotherly welcome. A separatist segregationist outcome is usual (Hill 1963).

The relative ease with which most Christians have been insulated from the awkward social implications of universalism contrasts with the stark dilemmas which faced settler congregations in the colonies. On the whole, they behaved with phenomenal indifference to the spiritual fate of the natives. Yet any condemnation of them for lack of proselytising zeal must be seen as somewhat hypocritical so long as it comes from home congregations secure in their homogeneous enclaves.

The proselytising zealots were the missionaries themselves, a group so distinctive that they invariably operated outside the existing framework of Christian organisation, constituting themselves into purposive societies. Their peculiar role placed them outside both home and settler congregations. Whereas home congregations regarded them with tolerant indulgence, seeing them as possibly heroic, settler congregations regarded them with suspicion and hostility, seeing them as agents of agitation and disturbance, creators of new social problems with which settlers would have to contend.

III

Settler congregations may be seen as facing four alternatives *vis-à-vis* the religious world views of the native population: they could convert them but organise them into segregated congregations; they could do nothing, out of indifference to the universalist injunctions; or they could reject the universalist doctrine. The alternative selected depended on a host of factors, demographic, economic, cultural, political. It also depended on religious factors themselves – factors of organisation, whether the church was hierarchic or democratic, whether religious functionaries were recruited locally or by immigration, were celibate or married. Theology was another variable, though one which proved flexible, depending on organisation and power to systematise the sacred world view.

Although the first option is the theologically expected choice, sociologically we would expect it to be rare, since it would be exercised only as long as the number of converts remained few enough not to threaten the social fabric of settler society. Since, however, the number of converts would be likely to rise precisely in proportion to the inducements offered (amongst which access into powerful settler networks must be rated high), it is not an option which would remain viable for long.

The second option was typical of settler situations, though usually deplored by the missionaries. Its frequency might be explained by a combination of settler indifference and missionary zeal, ensuring that though proselytising occurred, social segregation inevitably resulted. The missionaries embodied universalism; the constant clashes between missionary and settler may be taken as an index of settler rejection of its practice.

Analysis suggests that the missionary preference for the first option rests on the same sort of concern that led settlers to the third: missionaries were anxious to establish enclaves of like-minded people of which they could feel a part. The settlers already had such enclaves. While the missionaries maximised the rewards of proselytising to encourage its occurrence, the settlers consolidated their privileged ranks, if not by actively discouraging conversions, then by ensuring that they did not entail social integration. Settler behaviour constantly undermined the credibility of missionaries whose universalism was couched in the imagery of brotherhood. The relative success and popularity of independent missionary societies reflects the strategic advantages to missionaries of severing ties with settler denominations.

The fourth option, explicit rejection of universalism, is apparently theologically incompatible with Christianity, yet we find theological predisposition to exclusiveness in the doctrines of election and predestination fostered by Calvinism. It is not surprising to find these arch-Calvinist doctrines and arguments being resurrected in the theological legitimation of an exclusive concept of Christianity that has more in common with archaic tribal religions than with the historic or modern religions (Bellah 1964). Whatever else may attach to this option, it is likely to be exercised by the religiously fervid. It is a rejection of social integration, but it is also a rejection of the indifference and compromise that characterise the second and third options.

IV

The religion which the Afrikaners brought with them into the Kalahari was Dutch and Reformed in origin, though in two centuries of adaptation to local conditions it had undergone certain changes, despite a continuing link with Europe which remained until the mid-nineteenth century the sole source of its ordained pastors (Jooste 1959). In 1857 a major schism over the liberalising influence of Armenianism had resulted in the establishment of the pietist *Gereformeerde* church in the Orange Free State, while in the Transvaal a determination to be free of the Cape establishment had resulted in 1860 in the *Hervormde* church as the official state church of the northernmost republic. Hinchliff (1968) characterised the religion of these trekker republics as embodying 'a type of piety which was simple and direct, based upon the most literal application of biblical texts to the business of daily life . . . their Christianity was a religion of the household. It was patriarchal rather than sacerdotal.'

A more hostile contemporary reporter in the Free State in 1858 wrote:

> Most have no more than a kind of feeling or religious intuition, not based upon God's word because nine out of ten understand nothing of it, but base their beliefs upon all kinds of dreams and visions. . . . Some hold that the State Bible was made by the apostles and prophets exactly as it stood, border illustrations and all. . . . Others call it the work of pharisees if an unordained person leads prayer or conducts service. Some think themselves reincarnated and think therefore that they can sin no more because their sins have been forgiven them before they were born . . . many cannot read or write.
>
> (Pont 1959:89)

Sharing religion

The parallels between these white sectarians and the independent black African churches of the next half century are striking.

The *Gereformeerdes* were nicknamed *doppers*. The present *dopper dominie* of Ghanzi confessed uncertainty as to the derivation of the word. 'Perhaps because they cut their hair as though they had a *dop* (eggshell) over it, perhaps from *drompel* meaning threshold, because they were beginners.' He had however no uncertainty as to the meaning of the word.

> To say *dopper* is like to say *kaffir*. It's an insult. The *doppers* were despised. It meant that people were behind the times . . . they didn't want to go along with new directions. *Doppers* were cattle people. They needed to know how to go after cattle in the veld, and to do what was necessary in the house. The only reason they wanted to learn to read was to read the Bible and to count. . . . In those days if somebody started teaching geography or something about the stars he was chased away.

The earliest Ghanzi settlers were from the northern Cape and thus – nominally, at least – were members of the *Nederduitse Gereformeerde* church. Their links with the formal structure of the Cape church were very tenuous. We found evidence in a family bible in 1973 of the simultaneous baptism of five children in one family in 1916 by *Dominie* J. P. Joubert of Mafeking, suggesting long periods of separation from ordained clergy.

In 1920, however, there trekked into the Kalahari after four years in Lehututu a certain blacksmith, Theunis Kotze, sometime elder of the *Nederduitse Gereformeerde* in the desolate, flat, sheep-rearing area of Calvinia in the northern Cape, who had 'gone over' to the *Gereformeerde* church; a man of intense conviction, piety and fecundity, who was to establish the *Gereformeerde* congregation in Ghanzi. His fecundity alone would probably have assured the perpetuation of his denomination: he came with seven unmarried sons and three unmarried daughters. 'Kotze drew people after him mainly through marriage. Through marriage the *Gereformeerdes* became strong.'

Within two years he had acquired, for less than two shillings a morgen and on deferred terms, a 5000 morgen farm which had been abandoned by the earliest trekkers. He called it *Eersterus*, the first resting place. 'It was the first place we owned in our lives', recalled his son, now a weathered cattle drover nearing retirement. 'It was so cheap we paid it off quickly.' There he set about establishing the *dopper* congregation. In 1947 he gave two morgen of *Eersterus* as the site for a church, which in 1948 was dedicated and the congregation formally established as a parochial district (*wyk*) of Gobabis. Within five years Kotze had been buried in the small, fenced, family burial ground beside the church.

104

Having overlooked the formal transfer of title deeds of the two morgen to the *Gereformeerdes*, he failed to leave behind any lasting physical symbol of this thirty years' endeavour. The church, together with the rest of his divided estate, was sold to a Herero cattle farmer in 1972 and now stands derelict, a hundred metres from the mud and grass huts of the new owners, beside the empty farmhouse where once Kotze's prospective sons and daughters-in-law gathered for residential catechism courses.

This change of ownership of the church is accepted phlegmatically and unsentimentally by Kotze's descendants. In this intensely congregational religion church buildings are of little importance.

Confirmations used to take place during the annual visit of the *predikant*. 'Old Theunis Kotze used to ride with ox and wagon to the Republic to get a *predikant*, and later he got one from Gobabis.' These clerical visits were described as 'private'. The expenses were met by a congregational collection 'but never in church. All the years Kotze was alive there were no collections in the church. It wasn't allowed.' Since cash was rare this ruling was, however principled, also pre-eminently practical, and may have been designed to protect the members of the congregation from embarrassment.

Kotze is recollected as a 'strict man', 'very learned about the Christian life and about the stars', with 'a very big bookshelf full of his books', who 'always had a bible in his hand'.

The visits of the *predikant*, although significant, were but a minor part of the *doppers'* religious life. Every Sunday they would meet in one another's houses, to sing psalms accompanied on occasion on a pedal organ. To these services the Bushmen connected to the household were expected to come. Kotze's son said, 'My father never had special services for the Bushmen but he tried to explain the thing to them. He always gave our people [*ons volk*] a place where they could hear, somewhere on the side.' The present *dominie* confirms, 'It is the policy of the Afrikaner that when house prayers are said, the servants must sit in the kitchen and listen.' Bushmen in service expected likewise to attend the Bible reading after every evening meal, to which, on Sundays, 'all the neighbours would come'. However, Kotze was 'absolutely opposed' to missionary work amongst Bushmen.

The passive settler attitude to the religious fate of the Bushmen, exemplified in these social arrangements whereby Bushmen were exposed to Christianity but not encouraged into it, was not out of line with central *Gereformeerde* church policy on the issue of the conversion of the heathen. This was an issue which had taxed the church from its earliest days, and upon which every church member could be expected to have strong attitudes, since, in the frontier context, it impinged directly upon each of them. The policy of the church had been forged in a bitter dispute

105

with the first *Gereformeerde* pastor to have received his training by 'apprenticeship' within southern Africa rather than abroad, *Dominie* Venter, who in 1869 seceded from the church rather than abandon his doctrine that blacks bore the outward and visible sign of damnation and that to attempt to convert them was contrary to God's will and word. Venter's racial exclusiveness found fairly ready theological legitimation in the election doctrines of the arch-Calvinist divines of seventeenth-century Holland, from whom the nineteenth-century Reform movement in Holland and South Africa drew much inspiration (Pont 1959). However, the gentler doctrines of Armenianism prevailed, and Venter failed to attract any substantial following. Most *doppers* adhered to the more liberal *Gereformeerde* orthodoxy:

> concerning the converted Coloureds we confess one holy general church and holy community, and thus the converted Coloureds we regard as part thereof, as with any other converted nation. . . . But so far we do not see from the Word of the Lord that we must therefore let them share in the same social privileges. . . . By our present circumstances and insight we think that they should have separate services and should be cared for and led in their spiritual life in a separate manner. It is our longing that this should be done by the church itself, not by societies, or by so-called missionaries.[6]

A contemporary church member echoes this nineteenth-century policy: 'Now the Lord made us different, and the Lord said to his disciples "Go out and spread the Gospel to other nations." He didn't say, "Unify them". Each nation must be separately served and everybody must have services in his own language.'

However, the exclusiveness which Venter defended, which is the antithesis of universalism, probably remained more popular with the rank and file *doppers* than their faithfulness to the church establishment suggests. The Ghanzi community to this day exhibit a deep ambivalence to the issue of the conversion of Bushmen, unwilling to condemn the principle, but unprepared to assist the practice. Meanwhile, the establishment has moved cautiously towards racial integration, talking of 'the Christian duty of churches to educate their members for and in the practice of a healthy Christian communion of believers . . . neither race nor colour should exclude anyone from corporate worship' (Horrell 1957:21).

V

The practice of mission in Ghanzi began in 1963 when *Dominie* Kruger, who was a *Gereformeerde* missioner to Bushmen in Gobabis, acquired a morgen of land from the Ngamiland Trading Company at D'Kar to start a local mission station for Bushmen. *Dominie* Kruger, who was part-time *predikant* to the white congregation, may well have been influenced in this direction by the dramatic reduction in his white congregation at this time. Between 1961 and 1964 the white *Gereformeerde* congregation shrank by more than a third, to twenty-six families. Within a few months *Dominie* Kruger had acquired, from an emigrating farmer, and on behalf of the church, several thousand morgen at D'Kar, as mission farmland, in exchange for land at Aranos in South West Africa.

The white settlers watched the establishment of the mission with scepticism. White Afrikaans students from the University of Potchefstroom came in a vacation and built the mission church; white English-speaking students from the University of Witwatersrand came in their vacation and built the mission school. Yet, 'it went badly. We had difficulties. The work proceeded slowly because our people here didn't like the idea of a mission to the Bushmen. They didn't want to be bothered by the mission; more than that, they actually hindered it a lot.'

Local Afrikaner criticism of the mission was made at various levels. People deplored the fact that the missionary was a part-time absentee overseer, unable to speak Bushman languages, and that the full-time black evangelist manning the station slowly acquired but a halting command of one dialect.

> They ought to go about the mission more thoroughly, more reasonably. They mustn't come to us and ask us to interpret for them. There are lots of Bushman words that we ourselves don't know, and the Bible is very difficult to translate.

> Interpretation never works properly. It goes from Afrikaans to Setswana and from Setswana to Bushman, then it's quite altered. It's no longer what the *predikant* said. I know, because I know all three languages, and my wife also.

> There's few that can talk a Bushman language so well that they can really explain the things of the Lord to him.

Of their own fluency in local languages Afrikaners said; 'It's not surprising: we grew up with them.' But the missionaries, they argued, because they could not speak the language, did not really communicate with the Bushmen. They neither understood the Bushmen, nor perceived how little the Bushmen understood them.

> There are Bushmen who have been accepted into the church, who are members, who receive communion [*gebruik nagmaal*], but they haven't the slightest idea of what *nagmaal* means. He takes bread

107

and he eats, he takes wine and he drinks, but he doesn't know what it actually means.

In my opinion a Bushman understands one thousandth of what I understand. They haven't got the idea of what it means. The Bushman believes that there's a God in heaven, they've got a name for him and all. But the Bible is too far above him, too complicated. I myself cannot understand everything that is in the Bible if it's not explained to me by somebody cleverer than I.

Over and over again the congregation returns to the theme of meaning. The church community as a community of fellow believers must be composed of like-minded people. The very intimacy between boer and Bushmen in Ghanzi gives them the strongest assurance that they are indeed, in this respect as in many others, different. They are confounded by the sheer practicalities of inducting Bushmen into this Afrikaner world of the *Gereformeerde* fold, with its own Lord; for *die Here* (the Lord) is intimately acquainted with the vicissitudes of the Ghanzi daily life. He is invoked on numerous occasions, evoked as prime mover in history and as author of their biographies; He is slipped into conversations with an easy familiarity; He is the God of a numerically rather small and therefore intimately known people. The *dominie* at *nagmaal* has no hesitation about troubling Him with the particular needs of the Ghanzi community. Prayers are for the safe journeying of the children on the cattle truck that is to bring them from their boarding school in Gobabis the following weekend; for the quality of the religious radio broadcasts from South West Africa that they in their lonely farms will be listening to in the coming three months; and He is thanked that His people are not only bound to Him but to one another in a constant round of visits, upon which His blessing is invoked. There is profundity in somebody's jocular comment, 'All these churches! Sometimes I think they must each have a different god!'

When Afrikaners deprecate the capacity of the Bushmen to understand the 'things of the Lord', they are not engaged in any general belittling of their intellectual potential. These same people note the Bushman facility in mastering the principles of engines, the readiness with which they learn to repair windpumps – 'If you give them education we'll be working for them one of these days.' The point they are making is the more sociologically valid one, that religious ideas, above all others, deal in essential abstractions, the meaning of which arises out of the collective experience, and cannot be taught in isolation. 'I don't know how it is in your church, but in our church you have to learn to be a member before you can take *nagmaal*. But they simply take the Bushman and teach him *Our Father*. He learns *Our Father* and he understands nothing but he is accepted and he can take *nagmaal*. I am against that.'

The distinction between the ritual act and the non-ritual act is in the weight of symbolic meaning attaching to the former. The danger, as the boers see it, lies in the disjunction between the ease of outward conformity and the difficulty of sharing the invisible sacred cosmos without which the former is meaningless.

> A Bushman could very easily learn circus. If you take him to a circus he'll pick it up very quickly and be able to do it all. But concerning the things on the Lord's side, he still needs to be educated. The mission should have started by taking little Bushmen children and teaching them, so they could carry the thing on. But a fifty or a sixty-year-old Bushman, he learns nothing about it.

The boer conviction that the Bushmen's reception of Christianity is very different from their own is confirmed for them by the very high drop-out rate on the mission. In the thirteen years of ministration about fifty Bushmen have been accepted as communicant members, 'but those fifty are now dispersed over the whole of Botswana', according to the *dominie*. 'The Bushmen don't stay in one place, they move out, they move around everywhere. There's one of our members in Gaborone.'

Afrikaans church members say there are twenty-eight local Bushman members left,

> but lots of them are no longer active and the *dominie* no longer visits them. On the farm next to us there are two Bushman members and for years they haven't been to *nagmaal* or even been to church. Then the *dominie* says to us we must bring them to church. So we load them up and take them right to the church, but they don't attend the service. They go off and meet their friends.

This high rate of Bushman defection confirms for them the basic futility of programmes of premature proselytising and the wisdom of their own passive policy.

VI

Historically the *Gereformeerdes*, like all reformed Protestant churches, stand in the non-ritual tradition. But the particular historic circumstances of the southern African interior, the dispersed sparse population, the vast distances, have lent their one central ritual, *nagmaal*, a disproportionate significance. For many Afrikaners, it is still the only time they see a *predikant*; but above all it has always been the great coming together, the assembling and concentrating of the community which, according to

Durkheim (1915:470), is essential if the society is to 'become conscious of itself and to maintain at the necessary degree of intensity the sentiments which it thus attains'.

There are three *nagmaal* services. The preparation service on Saturday afternoon is a time of earnest self-examination; the prevailing mood is solemn and quiet as people await the *nagmaal* on Sunday morning, the climax of which is the ritual sip of wine from the common cup. This is followed by a more mundane meal outside the church to which the woman of each household usually makes a contribution. There is a noticeable cathartic relaxation, which is carried into the final Thanksgiving service later in the day.

Because each member is charged not to take *nagmaal* unless his conscience is clear, unless he has settled feuds and put wrong-doing behind him, the service has for its participants a heightened social interest. 'Of course they all go to church,' said a disillusioned emigré son of a Ghanzi farmer, 'they go to look and see who doesn't take *nagmaal*, and who does, and they gossip and speculate.' The social pressures to attend are compulsive. 'There are no people here who don't go to church. We go to church because there are so few people that if you don't go they ask you where you are.'

The *nagmaal* then acts as a social control, not only in the latent Durkheimian sense, but because to take *nagmaal* is explicitly to declare that you have adhered to the prescribed ethic. In this, too, the acceptance of Bushmen into the church creates problems for the boers.

> I myself I'll never do mission work. I know the Bushman too well. I have nothing against mission work. If you say you're doing mission work I will say you're better than me, but I myself, never! Now along comes the *predikant* from the other side [outside Ghanzi] who doesn't know any Bushmen; now they come along and put that Bushman at the *nagmaal* table. In the meantime he's the greatest rogue, *dronksuiper* [imbiber] and quarreller that you can get, that one, whom he puts at the communion table. The *predikant* doesn't know about it. In my whole nation the mission work is not done properly, that's the whole truth, it's not done properly. The man who supervises the mission, he must be a man who sees that this Bushman can take *nagmaal*, and that one can take *nagmaal* – not simply anyone taking *nagmaal*. That grieves me, it grieves me. He's the greatest rascal, he comes out of gaol in the morning and the next day is Sunday and he's there in church.

The prospect of converted Bushmen presented the white congregation with a new organisational problem in their hitherto homogeneous community. The democratic structure of the church had grown out of this homogeneity and demanded continuing homogeneity for its continued functioning. The segregation of mission congregation provided a temporary solution to the problem, but one with which the boers had always felt uneasy. 'When *Dominie* Kruger began this mission to Bushmen I said to him, "*Dominie*, you are beginning something. You are packing up the sticks for a big fire." And he said, "No, man, there will be consequences." Now he's gone, he's out of the business, and we sit here with the fire that's been lit.'

The 'lighting of the fire' was the government decision that the parallel Bushmen and boer congregations constituted a breach of its non-racial policy. The separate Afrikaans services, which since 1961 had been held in the makeshift chapel on the back verandah of the mission house at D'Kar, were in future to be held with the Bushmen in the mission church.

Afrikaner reaction was to intensify their regrets that a programme for the conversion of the Bushmen had ever begun, not to question the legitimacy of the government decision. 'Well, it's the law of the land, you can't go against it. I'm not against the law of the land. It's their land after all. I stand under the government. It's our duty to be obedient to the government. And the one who doesn't agree with the government is free to get out of the country.'

The government assumption that those who share a religion will share other things beside, and ought therefore to worship together, comes very close to the Afrikaner interpretation of the matter. Their uncomplicated reluctance to anticipate such sharing with the Bushmen lay at the heart of their original resistance to the mission. Seeing their religion as an integral part of their life and life style, they saw also the full implications of the attempt to convert Bushmen to it. The apparent shortsightedness of the missionary *predikants* to the consequences of the mission were locally derided as stupidity, hypocrisy and opportunism, an unwillingness to stand up to the more powerful black elite and its liberal policies.

The double standards employed by *predikants* in dealing with Bushmen were demonstrated in a conversation alleged to have taken place between the *Gereformeerde* missionary and a more sceptical visiting *Nederduitse Gereformeerde predikant*, who was alleged to have said, 'Listen, this Bushman, who is a member, if he leaves Ghanzi and goes to Gobabis, he must approach Gobabis congregation [a white congregation in Namibia] to be accepted, because he's a member, that Bushman, he's a member. Can he now be elected to the church board?' And the missionary replied, 'No, he's not mature enough yet.' The *predikant* said, 'Where do you come from? If you're a member you have a right to be a church board member. How can you say he's not mature enough? If he's not mature enough, why did you accept him as a member?'

Because *nagmaal* symbolises the Afrikaner community at its most intense, purged of deviants, reconciled, linked in solemn commensality about the *nagmaal* table, it was this ritual which became the focus of Afrikaner exclusiveness in 1973 when they confronted the government decree to integrate. 'As far as the mission is concerned, they can come and sit beside me. But I don't take *nagmaal* with him, never.'

The imagery of pollution (Douglas 1966) was repeatedly invoked. Through the common communion cup the community was rendered vulnerable to dirt and disease.

> If we use the church cup together with them then we'll all catch sickness. They're too dirty, that's what it is.

> We know every Bushman. We live here. We know what kind of sickness there is in that household and this household. I don't believe anybody will deliberately do something to endanger his health.

> I don't believe it will work out. I have nothing against going to church with them, but to drink out of the cup with them – that's wrong. The *dominie* says that if we are true Christians and proper children of *die Here* then we wouldn't run away from taking *nagmaal* with them, but it's okay for him, I don't think he would take *nagmaal* with them if he had to drink last out of the cup.

The symbolic rather than physical nature of the exclusion is underlined by a comparison with the acceptable intimacy of Bushmen in domestic service, where their firmly fixed role renders them innocuous. Similarly in trans-Kalahari cattle treks commensality of boers and Bushmen drovers is not unusual; once again the clear demarcation of group facilitates intimacy.

Religion has hitherto been an important criterion of group. In the 1930s common religion had legitimated marriage between whites and Coloureds in Ghanzi, despite the traditionally sharp distinction between them, though in the 1950s the colour criterion had re-emerged as a salient separator even of fellow believers.

Thus, although by no means the only criterion, religion has been a central element in identity, powerful precisely in its ability to enforce normative conformity, both explicitly in its ethical system and implicitly through the close social bonds forged by the literal requirement of congregation.

VII

The religion of the Afrikaners in Ghanzi, though Christian and Protestant, and hence formally universalistic and individualistic, displays many

Fig. 16. Trans-Kalahari cattle treck moving out from a watering point. (Reproduced by permission of Argus Africa News Service, Cape Town)

of the features of what Bellah calls 'archaic' religion, characteristics of tribal Africa. Religion, like many other aspects of their society, has evolved in a tribal direction, possibly in reponse to their constant confrontation with tribally organised others. There is the tribal emphasis on collectivity, the 'limitation of literacy to specially trained scribes', the retention by the political leaders of elements of religious leadership. 'There is little tension between religious demands and social conformity ... traditional structures and social practices are considered to be grounded in the divinely instituted cosmic order' (Bellah 1964). There is the same narrow recruitment by birth from an exclusive ethnic base. Religion is ascribed, not chosen.

Yet the links with a wider world of Christianity make for tensions, since the imperatives of the more universal church are formally very different. This universal church is represented by the *dominie*. His position in the group is accordingly highly marginal; boer attitudes towards him are highly ambivalent. Although he is treated with great deference and valued for his ritual function, his point of view carries less weight than that of local elders. Attitudes towards him are not dissimilar to those towards government officials. Like them he represents a powerful, important yet essentially alien authority, whom they prefer not to offend. He remains essentially the outsider. Together with other aspects of formal church structure, the church building, church finance, church committees, he is basically dispensable.

When a farmer said 'We can't *klaarkom* [get by satisfactorily] without church', he was using 'church' in Durkheim's sense of the united moral community who share beliefs and practices, rather than the formal structures of personnel and property.

The formal boer response to the government directive to integrate the mission was ready compliance through the dissolution of their congregation. Informally the directive will lead to the revival of the their traditional practice of worshipping from house to house. Their mood was not defiant, merely defensive. The government was in effect pressing for the impossible: the transformation of their identity.

Religion would seem to be a social possession, not indiscriminately shared, but, on the contrary, jealously cherished as a token of membership in an exclusive community. This emphasis is largely overlooked in contemporary sociological debate, which grapples with the idea that while religion may be analytically separable from other areas, it is not necessarily institutionally separate. Thus the apparent secularisation of modern Western society is interpreted as the passing of a particular religious form, rather than the passing of religion itself. Preoccupation with the contemporary Western situation obscures the more usual instance, historically and statistically, of religion as given, primordial, unchallenged – as much a part of identity as race, sex, kinship and nation.

Christianity, despite its universalism, is fitted over and again to this particularistic mould. The universalism of Christianity must be seen against a pervasive contrary pressure to exclusiveness. This characteristic is most forcefully seen amongst Christian settlers, since it is here that the dilemma of inclusion or exclusion is most starkly confronted, the more so as the native population diverges from the settler population.

The white Afrikaner cattle farmers of the Kalahari are unusual people in an unusual situation. In their uninhibited articulation of their dilemmas they bring into sharp focus the typical 'settler' dilemma over sharing of religion with the 'natives'. This in turn is simply a stronger form of a tendency to exclude the unlike, which has seldom been absent from congregational religions. Denominationalism and sectarianism are attempts to close ranks, to gain an exclusive religious possession, even when recruitment is by proselytising. Significantly, these phenomena occurred in Europe when new technology had violated the bounded parishes which had been the previous locus of religious social life.

A racial element in Afrikaner reaction to Bushmen cannot be denied. Nevertheless to dismiss Afrikaner resistance to the conversion of Bushmen as mere racialism is unhelpful oversimplification.

Extract from transcript of tape recording, Ghanzi, 1973

Speaker: White Afrikaans woman, aged about 40
   Occupation: heavy-duty truck driver
   Married, four children
   Place of birth: South West Africa
   Citizenship: Motswana

I came to Ghanzi in 1954 when I married Gert. It was much better than now, but this is still freer than South West. You can move. If you want to hunt you can hunt. It's a quiet place. In those days I was used to Windhoek. It took time to get used to the still life.

There have been many changes. In 1955 if a Bushman made you angry because he did not do his work, then you gave him a hiding and it was finished and done. But now you're not allowed to hit him and he's so conscious of that fact, whether you hit him or not he'll go to the police and say you hit him, and he's right, and you're wrong. In earlier times if you fell out with the people of this land then there was more justice. If you were guilty you were guilty, but now, whether you're guilty or not, if the Bushmen complain, you are guilty, even if they misrepresent the situation.

Previously Bushmen were Bushmen. Now you can do nothing with their

115

children. The only good workers are the veld Bushmen, but they only work till the rains start, and then they're back to the veld. Lots of veld Bushmen come to the farms in the winter, not all, but those that are used to whites. They come seasonally. But the Nharo never go back to the veld. They say they can't live without water like the veld Bushmen. And they crave tobacco and sugar and tea. I can understand Nharo and G/wi, but I only talk fluently in Setswana. My children can all talk the Bushman languages, and my husband who was born here can talk them all. The implosives and explosives in the Bushman language make it very tricky. When I was little in South West I could talk Makoko, but I've forgotten it all.

When we came here everybody had their own little lot of animals, and everybody struggled with their little bit of land. There were no loans for fencing or for boring, like in South West Africa. Every farmer knew that whatever was achieved on his farm, he achieved it with his own hands and labour; he didn't get help from the government or anybody else. There are people who are now rich who were then poor who have farmed themselves up in the world.

When I first came my husband worked in a trading store, and lived in a two-roomed corrugated iron house. I had two rooms on the farm, and at weekends he lived with me. Then he got a Bedford lorry and he employed a driver and started to ride transport, but in 1962 he gave up the store and started to drive himself. Then he got a second lorry and for three years we both rode transport in two lorries. My children were brought up in the lorry. The five and four-year-old would look after the baby and feed him while I drove. It was difficult, especially washing and drying nappies at night, and getting stuck in the Lake [Ngami], and the rain, and the children wanting food. But they grew up. The eldest is now sixteen.

We transport cream from Ghanzi to Gobabis, and bring back cattle feed to Ghanzi, and fuel to Maun, and we bring back the supplies for Ngamiland Trading Company to Ghanzi. We try to spend weekends at home before we go down to Lobatse with cattle on Sunday nights. We've been on the cream round for two years. Previously everybody used to cream, now only a few whites still do it. Before, cream was the main means of making a living for most people. As farming has become stronger people rely instead on selling *tollies* [immature oxen], and on selling cattle at Lobatse abattoir. Now there are only four white creamers, and some Coloureds. Most of the creamers are now Kalaharis and Damaras from Kalkfontein and Makunda. You load up the cream from cream stations. You ride around and pick up the cans, and on your return you put down empty cans. Everybody has a number. On the seventh of every month we bring back the cream cheques.

The other day a Damara assaulted me – he hit me – because of the cream cheques. This month the machine that stamps the numbers of the cheques was broken, and we didn't get cheques on the seventh, we got them on the fourteenth. When we were on the way to Gobabis the little kids tried to stop us at Makunda, but we didn't stop because it was late and the gates [frontier passport control] were going to close. On the return the policeman at the gate stopped us and said the Damara was waiting for his cream cheque. The kids stopped us again. Then he came and screamed at us, 'I want my cheque, I want my cheque', and he hit me, and he jerked open the truck door to get my husband who was just out of hospital, and wanted to hit him too. He said I was a *Maboera* [an Afrikaner] and a *Makhowa* [a white], and that this wasn't my country, and he'd show me what he was going to do to me. The case is coming up on Thursday. If he'd been a white man I'd get my own back. He wouldn't have dared to lift his hand on the South West side.

When the English government was here then the one could not say anything he liked to the other. Now if you just say anything to them [the blacks] they say, 'You're a white man, and this is not a white man's country.' It's not actually hard for whites but it's not nice for whites. It's not nice to stay in a country and pay all the taxes, and that sort of thing, and have to always hear that it isn't your country, it's their country. It gets anybody. This *is* my country, I immigrated here and now I'm a citizen of this country. But it's not something you hear from the educated people: it comes from those who know nothing. This land is hard to live in. If you can stick it out here and make a living, then you can live anywhere in the world. Whenever anything irritates me I want to leave Ghanzi, but when I have to go I'll go heavily out of this Botswana.

8

Boers, bureaucrats and blacks

I

Afrikaners provide a convenient object upon which tension and hostility can be projected, not only in South Africa, where they may collectively constitute a proper source of grievance, but across the continent and beyond. Stories of the same tenor as the Scotsman, the Irishman and the Jew indicate the unease which Afrikaners generate. The Afrikaner stereotype is summed up in the conundrum circulating amongst English civil servants in Botswana in 1973: 'Why is an Afrikaner like rope?' 'Because he is thick, twisted and hairy.'

Such anecdotes possess some of the power of myth to propagate and keep intact a world view in which Afrikaners are ignorant, brutish and stupid. Their strong sense of ethnic identity is seen as an integral aspect of this syndrome of backwardness. While the social sciences have pointed to the flexibility of man to changing circumstances, there remains an obstinate popular tendency to see Afrikaners as exceptional to this finding, their behaviour as fixed and immutable. The very fact that Afrikaners have tended to share a common environment has lent credibility to the idea that they are all alike, not least in the matter of racialism.

British attitudes towards Afrikaners in the nineteenth century were percolated through the colonial experience, in which they were found to be awkward, cunning, hostile and evasive. Twentieth-century colonial officials in Bechuanaland thus brought to the task of administering the Afrikaners not an open mind, but a set of historically conditioned preconceptions.

A similar set of preconceptions guided British attitudes to blacks. African societies were regarded as primitive, barbarous and sunk in a primeval darkness. 'Almost everything relating to their manner of life is very filthy and tends to debase and degrade' (Newcomb 1860:783). The lamentable condition of the blacks was the result of ignorance and superstition. They could not ultimately be blamed for either. As Philip had seen in 1828 'savages' could be taught industrious habits (1828:277). Although they behaved with 'disgusting shamelessness' and had 'only a few meaningless rites and superstitions which may be the ruins of some forgotten creed', they could clearly be uplifted (Newcomb 1860:783).

A particular disdain, indignation or moral despair was, however, reserved for those who had turned their backs on the European civilisation of industrious habits, and assumed the ways of the filthy and debased. 'The Dutch boers of South Africa' as early as 1847 had been depicted as 'virtually barbarians . . . scarcely less wild in their habits than the Hottentots themselves . . . filthy. . . Nominally Christian barbarians . . . standing proof that Protestants, and they too of Saxon blood, may drop out of civilisations and take their place on the same level of ignorance and social brutality with the barbarous tribes of the earth' (Bushell 1847).

In the last decade of the nineteenth century the German governor Leutwein in South West Africa had derided local boer adaptation to the interior as 'going kaffir'. Wealthy German settlers in the colony at this time used the terms 'going native' and 'going boer' as interchangeable descriptions of the same disturbing and retrograde renunciation of civilised European values (Bley 1971:110). In 1907 witnesses before the Transvaal Indigency Commission made constant reference to 'kaffirised whites'. 'They have been accustomed to loafing about at home and hunting. They really do not know what it means to put in a day's hard work.'[1] In the prevailing evolutionary framework, such behaviour epitomised degeneration. Those who lauded the wage labour ethic, encouraged thrift and decency, advocated modesty and championed virtue, condescendingly accepted the burden of uplifting the black heathen, vented on the essentially similar white boers all the fury and derision reserved for apostates.

The languages of black societies were regarded as curious, exotic; a certain kudos attached to their mastery; their orthography was an academic challenge; the emerging patois of the white pastoralists was mocked for its guttural crudity. The artefacts of blacks were evidence of a dark simplicity; of whites, evidence of abysmal backwardness. Blacks were lazy because they lacked the certain guide of true religion; whites lacked moral fibre.

II

By the second half of the nineteenth century the civilising influence of entrepreneurial missionary and speculator, already powerfully established in the south, was pushing into the interior. The Afrikaners on the periphery of colonial expansion experienced that influence as a threat to their economy and their culture. In specific rejection of all that it offered, they turned to the dry hinterland, preferring the freedom and uncertainty of the veld to what they perceived as the bondage of wage labour. The Ghanzi Afrikaners had been refugees from the settled, sober, hard-working routines of the emerging new economies of South Africa. In the Kalahari they were isolated from the pressures of progressive change which elsewhere in southern Africa were transforming the ethnic integrity of dispossessed and disoriented Afrikaners into a bitterly defensive racialism.

Amongst the British officials who came to administer the Ghanzi boers the stereotype of hopeless intractability was quickly verified. In 1913 'only four settlers in the District at present justify their existence. The remainder can be considered as poor whites.'[2] In 1920 the population was composed of 'numerous families of trekboers. These are merely squatters and content to live on the proceeds of a few head of cattle or pick up a job transport riding and taking out cattle, a class of work which suits them well.'[3] Like the Afrikaner indigents of the Transvaal in 1908, 'Some are simply squatters, usually on government land, eking out a precarious existence by raising a few mealies, hunting, ploughing for kaffirs, transport riding, or doing odd jobs for neighbouring farmers such as fencing, killing white ants, brickmaking, breaking in young oxen and cutting timber.'[4] In 1924 'the average mentality of the present population is extremely low and the district is rapidly drifting into poor whiteism',[5] a state always signally more alarming than poor blackism. By 1934 most of the farmers in Ghanzi were classified as 'paupers and squatters'.[6] After the district had been most seriously affected by the coincidence of foot and mouth disease with drought, followed swiftly by flooding and malaria, the District Officer recommended that those who had shown no thrift or failed to rally to the defence of the Crown in the Great War, should be denied relief unless prepared to pay for it in cattle. It was to the credit of the Resident Commissioner for the Protectorate that, although agreeing that 'the farmers there are a poor lot on the whole at any time', he insisted that he 'would not have these wretched people who are half starved given relief with one hand and made to hand it back with the other'.[7] Twenty years later another District Commissioner dismissed most of the Afrikaner signatories to a residents' petition as 'ne'er do well poor whites . . . born in wagons . . . illiterates . . . reputed to be mental . . . to drink heavily'.[8]

Adverse comments persist to the end of British rule. In the routine reports to their successors outgoing District Commissioners have left an eloquent, vivid and essentially negative image of the Afrikaner community. Their 'ambition is usually limited to the exercising of cunning to confound government and other farmers. Few farmers are prepared to do much hard work to better their farms and fewer are prepared to do any hard thinking . . . their capacity for cooperation is infinitesimal.'[9] There are reports of 'whispering compaigns which drive the more volatile to the Camp, filled with sounds and furies of varying emptiness'. However, 'most of their faults can be ascribed to a life of isolation, hardship and appalling monotony'. 'To describe them as farmers is to call chalk cheese. In actual fact they are miners, rather indolent miners, who take cows out of the land and certainly put nothing back.' 'On no account ignore them. You can scream at them, threaten them, or even kick their backsides, but on no account ignore them. As long as they feel that you are interested in them they will be happy.'

To officials was attributed all the very real power of the administration over the daily lives of the people. Officials responded with patronage, manipulation or mockery according to temperament. 'Never say anything good about one farmer to another. You will find that some farmers are more deserving than others. However, never let yourself be so misguided as to favour these *openly*; what they desire above everything is apparent equal treatment from the D.C. who is considered capable of performing miracles.' Officials did exercise their power to promote or thwart the interests of selected people, particularly in the vital matter of farm allocation, when a negative report from the District Commissioner – 'He lacks energy and initiative . . . in my opinion [there is] very little chance [of him] making a success out of any farming venture' – could effectively ruin a man. Little wonder that they believed that 'Government is all powerful and without benison out of sheer contrariness.' An old Afrikaner woman said, 'We learned that if you said you liked the Magistrate then he stayed. And if you said you did not like him then he stayed also, but a bit longer.' It is not surprising that 'almost without exception the farmers are most polite to government officials, particularly the District Commissioner'.

III

The pragmatism of the Afrikaners' polite and deferential public response to the colonial administration and its representatives has continued to characterise their relationship with officialdom in independent Botswana. The transfer of power to the black majority meant that Tswana officials assumed a very real power to determine the fate of Afrikaners. The relationship between farmers and officials is tellingly reflected in the phrase 'bow down' used by one man to describe the community's fearful anticipation of post-Independence status relationships. But not all anticipation of the transfer to black rule was negative. Asked what difference Independence had made, the answers of several poorer whites reflected dashed hopes, frustrated optimism: 'Everything is exactly the same.

Nothing has improved. We pay the same taxes on our lorries, we pay the same income tax. The British might as well have stayed.' 'The poor are poorer and the rich are richer.'

The Afrikaners' attribution of fearful power to officials is a reflection of their own powerlessness. There is a continuing debate in sociology on the relative strength of economic and political factors in the determination of power, with the Marxist orthodoxy of the primacy of economic factors contested in the Third World where sheer political office is frequently a route to control over economic resources rather than vice versa. The debate is often confused by the variety of scales envisaged by the debaters, whether power in a village, a faction, a metropolis, or in the arena of international affairs. The effective power of a local politician is not necessarily diminished by the shadow of a multinational corporation over his territory, despite large-scale theoretical conjecture by academics.

The two strands of power in Ghanzi are ownership of the land and high political office in whose gift the allocation of new state land lies, not directly, but indirectly through the creation and execution of policies determining citizenship and residence. Mere possession of a farm is not a guarantee of security since, for example, political offences can deprive one of possession by denying residence or citizenship. The potency of ownership lies, of course, in the wealth and independent bargaining power which ownership of this resource is generally reckoned to entail.

The first white settlers were granted *use* of Crown lands against an annual payment, on the understanding that the land would become freehold after thirty years. The exact stages in the collapse of this arrangement are obscure, but we read of the auctioning of abandoned Ghanzi farms in 1913, and it seems that one or two people with capital persuaded the government to sell outright before thirty years had passed; certainly those paying the annual £5 for 5000 morgen in the 1940s were never clear whether they were hire purchasing the farms or not, though the government were sure they were not. The quit rent contract expired in the 1930s with very few having completed purchase. The majority of farms remained Crown land, leased to a small shifting group of struggling, rent-evading stock keepers.[10]

The administration never ceased to grieve and wonder that the Ghanzi settlers had by and large failed to transform land into wealth. The decision in the mid 1950s to survey, fence and convert the entire Ghanzi block to freehold was a decision to force more intensive commercial ranching in the area. The problem of capitalisation through loans or bonds could not be resolved as long as farmers remained mere leaseholders, unable to offer any security.[11] In 1957 the work of surveying and redrawing farm boundaries excited new anticipation of private ownership. Competition for land, hitherto somewhat casually regarded as a communal resource, was under way. In January 1958 a visiting official found it

> very difficult to describe the atmosphere which exists at Ghanzi at the moment but I imagine it similar to that which prevailed on the eve of the gold rush earlier in the century, but that land, not gold, is the objective. Everyone is out for the best he can get for himself at any price and all are likely to be ruthless.[12]

In September 1959 the District Commissioner personally distributed prescribed forms of application to all residents, who were to get priority both in the allocation of farms and in the very easy terms for payment.[13] Each farmer had subsequently to appear before the European Land Settlement Board, a sub-committee of the newly established Land Board Commission, which met at Ghanzi. Clear terms for acceptance or rejection were never set out, beyond race and residence; scope for favouritism was undoubtedly wide. In the event only nineteen of the eighty-seven applicants were refused farms, some apparently because they had no capital, others because they had no sponsors.[14] Newness to Ghanzi also decreased chances: the so-called new trekkers were more than a quarter of all applicants, and more than half of the rejected. Those who, although new, were kinsmen of established residents, fared better than those with no relatives.

In the stringent conditions which attached to the purchase (adequate stocking, fencing, boring, and the reduction of the farmers' households to acceptable British levels),[15] the local officials acted as watchdogs for the Crown.[16] The Crown's right, if conditions were breached, to declare the property to be 'forfeit . . . to eject every occupier therefrom',[17] was withdrawn in 1964, but not before at least one unsuccessful owner had been dispossessed.[18]

The motives behind this legal pressure against the poor were never clear. British colonial policies in territories with significant indigenous populations often appear to have operated on the assumption that socio-economic discrimination was a satisfactory alternative to ethnic discrimination; but at the same time there was a concern that whites maintain a standard of living such that they were in no danger of being part of the inferior majority. In principle there was a rule of non-racialism; in practice a considerable effort was made to ensure that legitimate socio-economic distinctions coincided with more traditional ethnic distinctions.

IV

Independence did not create any immediate revolution amongst the Afrikaners who remained in 1966 to celebrate it. The poorer and prouder had already left. Some who had been refused farms under the British hung on to try their credentials before new Tswana officials. The policy of non-racialism had very little impact on the established relations between ethnic minorities of the district, whose distinctiveness was firmly legitimated in cultural terms which embraced physical differences as easily as differences in dress, language and housing style. 'The equality ruling simply came in without our noticing it. It was just as it was before.'

The one conspicuous change was in the civil service, where Tswana from the east now dominated the upper echelons, replacing the British who had previously made the powerful decisions about mortgages and tax payments, export and residence permits, land allocation, citizenship, innocence and guilt. Behaviour towards this section of the population was deferentially modified, as it was to those others who, though not in office, were seen to have influence in the new administration. 'If you invite them [officials] to come in and sit down, they come in and sit, but if you don't invite them, they remain outside. Say for example a big man comes, say the Magistrate or veterinary officer; now he comes in, he sits down, you give him tea. In this way we get on well, with politeness.'

Relationships with other groups had likewise varied with circumstances before Independence. The nineteenth-century *de facto* power of the Tswana had promoted careful circumspect relationships between established blacks in the interior and small parties of Afrikaners who had ventured into their territory. Under the impact of powerful British intervention, seen as favouring black over Afrikaner interests, attitudes towards blacks became periodically more defensive, competitive and hostile, particularly over the question of allocations of land. In 1936 and 1937 there had been sharp disagreement between the Ghanzi settlers and the District Commissioner, whose recommendation that Damaras and Barolong be settled on the north-eastern periphery of the farming block met with the reproof of the Government Secretary who wondered 'whether it would not be asking for trouble' to bring these 'admittedly not too law-abiding natives' near to European settlement.[19] The District Commissioner replied that 'Damaras and Barolong are on the whole the higher class of natives in Ghanzi and the most law-abiding',[20] overlooking the legitimacy of the complaint made by a farmer the month before that 'Picannin is sinking a well south east of Tswaai between Tswaai and SeKobas pan. Sir, I don t think this is right because more natives will avail themselves of the same opportunity thinking they have a perfect right to squat there.'[21] In 1937 a petition supported by thirteen signatures asked for 'native farmers to be moved forty miles from the nearest white farm', since 'natives are somewhat careless in regard to their own farming operations and do not as a rule care much about the general welfare of their surroundings, and consequently, their presence, wedged in between

124

Fig. 17. Black civil servants in Ghanzi Camp

as they are at present, is certain to retard the beneficial development of our farms'.[22] The administration had already interpreted the farmers' concern more cynically, as 'their probable inability to graze stock on Crown lands, for which they pay no taxes, in the event of persons settling in the immediate vicinity of their farms'.[23]

In the 1950s Afrikaner political triumphs in the south, brought close to Ghanzi by the wave of immigration and the increasing use of trucks, suggested a new shape for Afrikaner identity. Against the long accustomed self-image of misunderstood, politically impotent, inferior underdog, loomed a tempting and masterly alternative. At the European Advisory Council meeting in 1954 the incorporation of Ghanzi into South West Africa was urged. But the winds of change were blowing in a very different direction, putting power directly and firmly into the preponderant black hands. Ghanzi Afrikaners rapidly readjusted their view to accommodate the new circumstance. 'You know, for us who were born here, who are white, it's very difficult to extend their hand to a black and say, "Good day." Or perhaps you're in the [witness] box, to say, "Your worship" or "Mister" or "Missus". But you must do it.' Deliberately, wilfully, with calculation, they set aside outdated norms in a conscious effort to meet the new demands.

V

Afrikaner relationships with each of the other local groups differ. Objectively they differ in terms of relative dependence and independence, similarity of life style, physical proximity, and in the sheer number of social bonds sustained between members of the groups; subjectively they differ in the attitudes and images held. Afrikaners distinguish Makoko from Nharo Bushmen, and Nharo from G/wi and G//ana. They attribute to each very different characteristics. They think of Bamangwato and Bangwaketse rather than the collective Tswana. They single out the Barolong and the Batawana for special consideration since these are the Tswana groups with whom they have been in closest and longest contact. They can go further and distinguish the various ethnic groups with whom they have had contact in Angola and in Namibia, and the various Bushman groups from the south west and the swamps of the Okavango.

The sensitivity of the Afrikaners to groups and subgroups is the outcome of their experience in situations where ethnic identity has been a cardinal principle for the structuring of the social relations in which they have been involved. Their attitude contrasts with the prevailing metropolitan tendency to characterise in terms of black and white, perhaps an instance of Simmel's typology of metropolitan man who of necessity numbs himself to the variety of stimuli which the metropolis presents, deliberately indifferent to all but a few selected symbols. The contrast is with the small intimate community where everybody is known. Strangers, black and white, are conspicuous to all in Ghanzi.

Relationships with the Herero exemplify Afrikaner adjustment to a prosperous non-Tswana black minority. The Herero are successful cattle people who have for years vied with the boers for access to grazing, not only officially through competition in the allocation of land, but unofficially on the unallocated Kalahari veld where from time to time both groups have been known to sink illicit wells, usually in the hope that possession would confer eventual rights to ownership. Afrikaner attitudes to and relations with Herero, whom they call Damara, are shaped by this circumstance. The Herero are depicted as smart dealers, on the make, well-connected, arrogant. 'The Damaras are very shrewd. One comes here with nothing and within a few years he's a rich man.'

Certain of them came to be known to various farmers through cattle trading, by name, face to face.

In 1973 an Afrikaner sold part of his farm to a 'half Herero' who had considerable cattle and land-holdings in the west. The earlier antipathy to sharing Ghanzi with black cattle-keepers has melted into an acceptance of racially mixed occupancy and a willingness to profit from the new pattern: 'there was no feeling amongst the Afrikaners against it [the sale of the farm], not at all'.

Intimate recollections of Herero vary from the macabre ('In 1964 my father's brother was murdered by Damaras while riding transport from Walvis Bay to Ghanzi. They cut him limb from limb till he was dead.') to the intimate friendliness of dependence ('We had nothing, and an old Damara on the South West border lent us a span of oxen to trek back to Ghanzi in 1946; that was how we started, from scratch.' 'At the time [1904] my parents were living at Ghanzi and the Damaras who were fleeing from the Germans stopped there and my parents fed them. Some of them were nearly dead with hunger. Then the Damaras went to Ngamiland and my parents went with them.')

Against this background the standard social distance question 'What would you think about having a Damara to a meal?' might well elicit a scandalised, 'What! Here? In *my* house? Never!' Actual behaviour in this matter is different. Three local Afrikaner farmers live with common law Herero wives, and everybody in the district now accepts that occasionally Herero cattle dealers will eat at the communal trestle tables put up by the Afrikaner women to cater at the quarterly cattle sales. 'And if he's a well behaved person and clean we do not mind.'

There must also be local recollections of the communal meals in earlier decades. Bley in his history of South West Africa at the turn of the century describes the heavy economic dependence of Afrikaans trekkers on the Herero headmen, 'all of which meant that the claim, demonstratively made by the Herero ruling class, to be of at least equal status with the Europeans, simply had to be accepted' (Bley 1971:88). The whites turned necessity into a virtue and 'assiduously cultivated these relationships despite prevailing views on white supremacy' which offered them a unique chance of access to 'African if not European upper classes'. Bley also comments on white farmer participation in African celebrations, and the 'amazing amounts of discussion that took place in such circumstances'. The half-Herero Coloured descendants of these particular settlers bear their names in Ghanzi today.

Not all social exchanges are marked by courtesy, consideration and good feeling. A Kgalagari employee who was, it subsequently transpired, about to displace an Afrikaner employee as headman on a farm, reported the following conversation between them while repairing a truck:

127

Fig. 18. Domestic cooperation. Catering at the quarterly Ghanzi cattle sale

Afrikaner: Why does the hair of you kaffirs grow so short?
Kgalagari: No, I don't know.
Afrikaner: It's because you haven't got any thoughts in your head.
Kgalagari: There's no such thing!
Afrikaner: It is so. That's why your hair is so short. You'll always be
    stupid. Short hair, short thoughts.
Kgalagari: And your hair?
Afrikaner: My hair is long because my thoughts work such a lot.
Kgalagari: My hair may be short but the thoughts are not short.
    They work nicely.
Afrikaner: You're too black to get to the Lord. You'll never reach
    Him. You can't fly. You'll go to the Devil. You'll fall like a stone.

Offensive racialism is one aspect of this exchange. We should not let it
obscure other aspects: the patent sense of insecure inferiority of the
Afrikaner (as it turned out, well founded despite his formal status

128

superiority); the tolerance of the baiting by the Kgalagari, the shared naivety of the arguments, the immediacy of the interchange. It illustrates Afrikaners at their worst. An attitudinally very different yet situationally very similar incident was reported by a Bushman woman, who came to blows in argument with her white employer, to whom she had been attached since childhood as a *matie*. The two women, Bushman and boer, were grappling on the floor pulling each other's hair, when the husband of the Afrikaans woman came into the room. 'He laughed. He laughed and laughed. He wouldn't do a thing, he just stood laughing at her till she stopped.'

VI

Sociological scepticism about the value of attitude studies rests partly on a commitment to analysis at the level of actions rather than dispositions (Cohen 1966), and partly on the demonstrated irrelevance of many measured attitudes to subsequent actions. In the sociological literature on race relations the mere appearance of the term 'attitude' has become an index of a certain micro-sociological perspective, rooted in a model of society which is individualistic and ahistorical, associated with an approach which is reformist, and superficial in the sense that it is concerned with the apparent, the manifest, in contrast to the more fundamental structural concerns of the macro-sociologists. The particular circumstances which have brought about this polarisation could doubtless be traced. Sufficient here to suggest that to disregard attitudes is to disregard one of the most central aspects of our social nature; that many of the key terms of sociology, ideology, legitimation, false consciousness, are, on analysis, attitudes writ large. The difference between persuasion and coercion is *inter alia* the difference in attitude of the manipulated. The difference between rebellion and submission is likewise a difference in attitude.

The poor regard in which attitudes as social data are generally held may additionally be blamed both on the methods which have been used to elicit them and on the kinds of arguments they have been used to defend. The heyday of attitude studies was the 1940s and 1950s in the United States of America, where social scientists strove to achieve scientific credibility through the elaborate application of sophisticated statistical techniques to fundamentally questionable data. Much attitude measurement has taken place in a contextual vacuum, and the frequent finding that verbalised attitudes are not significantly correlated with behaviour becomes a source of puzzlement about the nature of man, rather than a criticism of research procedures which reduce so complex a phenomenon to a word game played in the informant's head.

Social psychologists have addressed themselves seriously and with ingenuity to the problem of attitude components and their inconsistency (Fishbein 1967, Thomas 1971). Sociologists have usually been content with cruder indices of race attitude (Pettigrew 1960, van den Berghe 1962). Inconsistency in sociological studies has been obscured by the preoccupation in most research with the classification of the measured population into the prejudiced and the unprejudiced, and the entailed search for the correlates of racialism. The standard technique is through the application of scales which measure for the presence or absence of 'liberalism' – in the sense in which the term has been used by Adorno *et al*. (1951) to denote a particular style of tolerant individualism – to which any kind of collective ascriptive discrimination is abhorrent, particularly on racial grounds. This ideological element in most sociological tests tends, we suggest, to trigger an ideologically consistent response, obscuring inconsistencies which might surface. It is well established that the interview or test situation is itself a social confrontation between tester and tested (Phillips 1973:17–37). While the more sophisticated researcher attempts to transcend this confrontation, others are often content with data solicited in confrontation, biased as they may be towards satisfying or thwarting the tester, according to context. A partial explanation of the high scores achieved on conventional social distance ratings by Afrikaans-speaking subjects in South Africa (van den Berghe 1962, MacCrone 1965) can be found in their repudiation of the perceived liberalism underlying the questionnaire.

Racial attitudes and social distance in Ghanzi are part of a situation in which the various groups are well informed about one another. Antipathies are rooted not in misconceptions but in real competition and conflict over scarce resources of various kinds. That there has hitherto been so little antagonism or conflict probably reflects the relative abundance of resources and the small compass of local ambitions, black and white. The new evaluation of Ghanzi veld as an economically valuable resource may sharpen conflict in the future. Stereotypes, which loom so large in social psychological studies of race as misinformed prejudice, play little part in Ghanzi, where familiarity and intimacy are the norm. Images of other ethnic groups are derived from shared specific experiences with particular people. The growing intrusion of outsiders into Ghanzi, as administrators, developers and entrepreneurs, promises the new intrusion of stereotypes, derived from other contexts and entailing new strains.

The Kalahari Afrikaners' race attitudes, as inferred from spontaneously expressed opinions and accounts and demonstrations of interracial interaction, display all the apparent inconsistency we would expect from people caught up in a suddenly changed situation. The slight edge which the local white minority had over the local black minorities during white rule has been reversed. The black majority, the Tswana, always economically and politically powerful, are now more powerful. The position of the Bushmen has been marginally redefined by expressed governmental determination to defend and assert their rights. The old ideology and the new, ethnic exclusiveness and non-racialism, exist side by side in an uneasy truce. Afrikaners feel themselves subject to very different expectations in different situations. Each ideology militates against the full expression of the other. In situations where listeners are perceived to approve of racial segregation, people describing their relationships with other groups carefully stress that, despite intimacies, they were never *kaffirboeties* (brothers of the blacks), a term by which liberals have always been contemptuously dismissed. When they perceive their audience to be sympathetic to non-racialism, they carefully stress that despite their concern to be separate, they were never racists.

Government has long been regarded by the Afrikaners as a regrettable necessity. It has always been something distant, something enacted on the far side of the Kalahari, represented with varying authenticity by the Magistrates who were also the District Commissioners. Abstract questions of political policy, abstract notions of independence or self-determination, have little meaning to them except as particular decisions enacted at the local level. Their evaluation of Independence is couched in practical not ideological terms.

They were gratified to realise that the new black Magistrates were cattle people like themselves, hard on Bushman cattle thieves, sharing Afrikaner outrage rather than British sentimental sympathy for hungry hunters. The reality of cultural proximity between Afrikaners and the new officials provides a relative security against contempt for their acculturation to local conditions. Even in far-away England we had been told how Afrikaners in Ghanzi, when their trucks finally broke down, would harness mules or donkeys to them, and sit behind the steering wheel, driving. The implication was less that they were too ignorant to repair them and more that they were too foolishly proud to relinquish the driving seat. Black officials, unaccustomed to affluence, and socialised to adaptations of this kind, appreciate the advantages of steering a drawn wagon, and find no humour in the practice which is common amongst blacks.[24]

It would be entirely false to suggest that there are no moments of confusion, no anxieties about black rule. Economic and political changes are seldom smoothly accomplished, even where ethnic and cultural differences are absent. The prevailing disdain of the elite Tswana for the boers is in part an inability to see them except as an outpost of the political Afrikanerdom of the Republic of South Africa. It is also tinged with envy:

Fig. 19. Adaptation: a poor Afrikaner's truck chassis water cart hauled by a donkey team. The steering is invaluable for holding the cart firmly in the deeply cut *spoor*

British race zoning policies during the Protectorate have given white farmers of Botswana, most of whom are Afrikaans,[25] a head start in the present scramble for freehold land tenure. The accusation that Afrikaners own a disproportionate share of the land wealth is not without substance, although in Ghanzi this is the direct consequence of policies which seem to have been designed to drive away all but the landowning few. The coincidence of the world-wide upswing of beef prices with Independence has certainly brought many Ghanzi farmers a new affluence,[26] for which, with charming naivety, they credit the government.

Confrontations between Afrikaners and officials are a mutual challenge. Afrikaners respond with tightly calculated concessions both to the new rules and to the novelty of authority in the hands of people unaccustomed to it. Afrikaners are under a new surveillance for any signs of racialism. A particular sensitivity has been developed by the administration to possible boer exploitation of the Bushmen. The Tswana's own traditional relationship with the Bushmen has been accompanied by the kind of attitude typical of a situation of great inequality of status, which ten years of officially endorsed non-racialism has not yet been able to

132

change. Popular Tswana attitudes towards Bushmen are still very super-
cilious, and there is scattered evidence of hardened prejudice towards
them, not least in the legal ruling that to call somebody Masarwa, the
name by which Bushmen in the service of Tswana in the east have always
been known, is itself evidence of racial insult. Officials implementing the
non-racial policy thus bring their own guilty heritage with them. They are
quick to recognise amongst Afrikaners that sense of superiority with
which they are so familiar, and quick to see evidence of racial discrimination on the part of a group amongst whom racialism is so important a part
of the stereotype.

In 1973 a local Afrikaner was prosecuted under the 'racial insult'
legislation. It was alleged that he had called a woman in his employ
'kaffir'. Because he was one of the new trekkers from South Africa, he
had been one of the last to apply for Botswana citizenship, which had not
yet been granted. A conviction might have meant refusal of citizenship
and consequent loss of his farm. He engaged a defence lawyer from South
Africa, which local Ghanzi officials interpreted as resistence to the spirit
of the law. An experienced, neutral (white, English) Magistrate was
specially co-opted to match the lawyer. The Afrikaners interpreted the
trial as a determination on the part of the administration to 'get' them:
'It's not that we want to beat the blacks, but we want justice. He did not
say it!'

Despite a very high level of Afrikaner concern about the case, only a
couple of Afrikaner men attended the hearing, one of whom came in an
almost representative capacity on the part of the others 'because I can
speak all three languages and I can check how it goes in the translation;
sometimes it goes very badly from the one to the other'. The Afrikaners
sat on one of the three rows of hard, backless benches provided at the
back of the court room for the public, amidst barefooted Bushmen
awaiting the trials of friends for cattle theft, and the black-skinned,
straight-nosed Hereros in blazers and flannels, friends of witnesses in
later cases, and off-duty Kgalagari clerks from adjacent offices. The
accused's wife waited anxiously at the local store with other wives and
several Afrikaner men, speculating on the case and its possible outcome
and implications.

The determination and sophistication of the prosecution was
thoroughly thwarted by the naivety of their chief witness, whose evidence
that the racial insult had been to herself in particular was that the accused
had addressed her by name before uttering it. Pressed for his exact words,
she suggested that he had said, 'Mrs Bokae, you kaffir'. This stretched the
credulity even of the prosecution, and brought a smile to the faces of the
Afrikaners present, among whom terms of respectful address are not
offered to employees. 'He called you missus?' asked the defence. 'Why

did he call you missus?' 'Because he respected me' came the coy reply. The Afrikaner was acquitted.

A case the next day against a Herero who hit an Afrikaans woman passed without Afrikaner notice or concern. Her husband and four children, dressed in their Sunday best, attended the hearing, a complicated affair with several interpreters laboriously rendering the proceedings from English to Tswana to Afrikaans to Herero and back again. Her assailant was found guilty and fined ten rand. There was no official reaction to her evidence that the Herero had said as he assailed her that she was a 'bloody boer', a 'white', and that he was going to 'fix' her. Not all racial insult is equally salient to the state. Nor are all attacks on Afrikaners equally salient to the Afrikaner community.

Paradoxically, the policy of non-racialism, which seemed so threatening in 1963, had by 1973 been transformed in the Afrikaner estimation into their guarantee of equal rights in a world in which opinion about the rights of whites was hardening fast. The very newness of the state lends its policies an air of fragility. A change of government could mean a change for the worse. Many are pessimistic, but not all. Asked whether he thought Afrikaners were secure from dispossession, one of them replied, 'As far as I understand the Bechuanas it won't happen. We have been a long time in the land and they are very good to us.' But this evaluation rests on politically naive evidence: 'When we're on the road and in trouble, they'll never pass us by. And we do the same for them.' Yet political sophistication is increasing with the grasp of new political reality. When Afrikaners say they are Batswana they know that, in terms of Tswana traditions as opposed to new democratic parliamentary system, to acknowledge political sovereignty of Tswana leaders is not to gain equality with the dominant group, but rather to acquire secure social and economic rights. Politically, Afrikaner ambitions are negative – to avoid trouble, to maintain the status quo. Their interest in the newly created District Council as so slight (despite the return of the appropriate quota of white farming representatives in the election) that very few knew anybody who was on it, nor what its purpose was.[27] Language is just one obstacle to Afrikaner participation in such committees.

It remains to be seen whether the traditional Tswana acknowledgement of loyalty can be broadened to embrace a traditional enemy.

9

Prospect: whites in a black state

I

The political problems of polyethnic societies are legion. The liberal solution, the pretence that there are no ethnic differences, has only very recently had its ethnocentric weaknesses exposed; in practice non-racialism is frequently fraudulent, since those belonging to or willing to acculturate to the dominant group outpace all others. The various ameliorative poverty programmes in the United States of America and Britain are for the most part inspired by the ideal of assimilation to the middle-class life style. Egalitarian ideals are satisfied by the provision of weighted handicaps in the competition for bourgeois prizes of higher educational opportunity and highly paid employment.

The adoption by Botswana of a liberal, non-racial, national policy in 1966, just as illusions about liberalism in American and Britain were beginning to fade, was a bold step.[1] If ethnicity was proving a tenacious factor in industrial societies, where its intrinsic irrelevance to the system could be argued, how much more tenacious it would be likely to be in a non-industrial society in which ethnicity had hitherto been the corner-stone of administration and organisation. Many factors contributed to the decision: the liberal British influence on decision makers; the necessity to be seen to be opposed to South Africa ideologically despite heavy depen-dence on South Africa economically; and the preponderance of Tswana in the composition of the population which ensured that for most people the policy would be without impact.

For the Afrikaners in Botswana the policy had immediate and intended impact in its forceful contradiction of separateness upon which their culture, so long in contact with alien others, had hinged. Practically, too, the policy had immediate impact in the decision to desegregate the schools, threatening Afrikaners with a radical disruption of their ethni-cally cushioned life style.

But the first ten years of independence have proved non-racialism a paper tiger. It has become for Afrikaners the banner under which they legitimately press for the retention of their rights as citizens, albeit white citizens, in a black state. They compare non-racialism favourably, not so much with white racialism in the south (though they are quick to point to their long-term security in Botswana as against the uncertainties of present and pending racial confrontations in neighbouring territories), as with anti-white Africanisation movements to the north.

Independence formally confers equality on the traditionally egalitarian relations between Afrikaner and Tswana by denying their separateness. Informally Afrikaners see their position as collectively precarious, not least because the collective definition in itself runs counter to the prevailing ideology, and thus renders their position precarious. Formally Afrikaners in Botswana have everything to lose and nothing to gain by insisting on their collective identity. Informally the situation is more complex: the Tswana tradition is of the slow and unequal political incorporation of alien ethnic groups. There is evidence of the tenacity of the ethnicity of the groups thus incorporated.[2] To this tradition the British, during the Protectorate, added the colonial complication of special privileges for whites, which, with Independence, has had repercussions in a popular wish to deny opportunities to whites.[3]

Afrikaner familiarity with the unofficial role of ethnicity in Botswana cautions them in their response to the contemporary situation. The many instances of their compliance with non-racialism is an index of their flexibility, a flexibility which is underlined by the discovery that they have not by any means been converted to the liberalism which underlies that policy. In this their response is probably typical of other ethnic groups in Botswana: the common people capitulate to a policy which is for the most part too remote to resist, and which can be strategically sidestepped if it impinges too directly. Non-racialism is the policy of the modernised elite who have already abandoned their particular cultural traditions for the Western liberal individualistic inheritance.

Thus the Afrikaners of Ghanzi have opened the membership of the Ghanzi Farmers' Association to all races and invited the Vice-President of Botswana, who acquired freehold in Ghanzi in 1964, to become its honorary president. Thus they have accepted the transition from British to black administration as the substitution of one set of outsiders by another, praising their sympathy as cattle people, deprecating the arrogance of some officials in their unaccustomed roles of power and influence; thus they continue to drink at the Kalahari Arms, now sharing the counter or the lounge with the few blacks acculturated to this new form of sociability. Catering at the quarterly cattle sale has become desegregated in principle, though in practice most blacks patronise black entrepreneurs, whites patronise whites – in either case food is prepared in cauldrons over fires in the open. They apply for citizenship, register as voters,[4] and pin posters of Seretse Khama on their walls.

In insisting on their right to opt out of multiracial schools and churches they show a fine sense of the importance of these particular agencies of socialisation. Afrikaner identity is still seen to rest on control of these areas. Their ambitions extend no further. 'We are Batswana', they insist, though even as they say it they are pessimistically calculating that they will be discriminated against as Afrikaners. They are not yet ready to abandon the informal Afrikaner identity which underlies the newer identity of citizenship.

Contemporary sociology often portrays ethnicity as something to be put on or shrugged off – preferably to be shrugged off, in accord with some loosely postulated principle of the progressive individuation of society. The social transition which preoccupied nineteenth-century scholars, and which they variously depicted as status to contract, ascription to achievement, has taken on moral overtones in contemporary sociology: ascription, particularly ethnic ascription, must yield to achievement.

Rational, calculating, profit-maximising man is at the heart of this sociology. While he may be intellectually reassuring, he is far too cerebral to serve as a model for Tom, Dick or Harry, let alone Thabu, Japie and Kashe. He is a Western cultural product. His very existence is at odds with another sociological principle, that we are born into a continuing social structure, whose definitions, norms and prejudices we must accept before we are able to think or to reject.

Ethnicity in this contemporary view is reduced to a strategy, adopted so long as it succeeds. Popular Marxism, with its assumption of material interests as prime mover, lends apparent support to this view. Thus the ethnic exclusiveness of the Afrikaners of South Africa is assumed to require no explanation, since the advantages flowing to them from their particular policies of racial separation would seem to offer a ready explanation in themselves. The persistently disadvantaged position of the Afrikaners at Ghanzi suggests a certain inadequacy in an explanation of this sort, which fails to take into account the staunch ethnicity of underdogs.

Barth's primordial ethnicity (1969) seems more plausible as the dominant model, the normal human condition. When race becomes intertwined with culture, as it does with remarkable consistency even in the labile industrial world, then the optional element in ethnicity becomes even less likely. There is, of course, no intrinsic connection between race and culture; but historically the probability that those we talk to, see and marry will be physically as well as culturally like ourselves is very high. For most people ethnicity is a 'given', the mutability of which they never entertain. Race matters because most people have learned to see their group in terms which *inter alia* include race. Societies differ in the extent to which they use race or ethnicity as a basis for organisation, even as they vary in the extent to which they use gender. There will doubtless also always be those who are teased by the balance between intrinsic and extrinsic determinants of social characteristics, for both gender and race. For the sociologist this balance is unimportant. The socially ascribed identitites are in themselves sufficiently well established and socially real for his particular level of abstraction.

The sociological response to race is in marked contrast to the anthropological response, a difference which would seem to be rooted in the very different contexts in which they have traditionally worked. The anthropologist is the stranger, who politely suspends his cultural prejudices in deference to his hosts, as he penetrates their alien world which he attempts to portray in its own terms. The Afrikaners of Ghanzi might be described in the anthropological mode as a tribe of cattle pastoralists, endogamous, with strong primordial sentiments, wary of strangers though elaborately hospitable, whose elders are anxious to maintain traditional socialisation, initiation and magico-religious practices upon which they see their continuity resting.

The sociologist has been trained to perceive the situation in rather different terms. Racialism, ethnocentricism, exploitation, domination, discrimination – the sociological vocabulary precipitates judgement. Whereas whites 'exploit' Bushmen, the Kgalagari have a 'feudal relationship' with them (A. Kuper 1970; Kuper and Silberbauer 1966).

II

Van den Berghe (1969:76–7) has suggested a formula for democratic rather than despotic pluralism. Racial despotism, he argues, will be averted when five conditions are met: (1) a low degree of cultural pluralism; (2) a high degree of consensus about procedural norms of government, probably with formal or informal quotas ensuring the representation of all groups; (3) a generally shared sense of the legitimacy of pluralism, possibly with specific counter-acculturative norms to ensure the continued integrity of groups; (4) a similar level of technological and scientific development by constituent groups; (5) cross-cutting cleavages, in particular a lack of coincidence between language, religion, political party, social class and ethnic group. The *de facto* pluralism of Botswana invites its rating on these criteria.

Culturally there is considerable similarity in Afrikaner, Tswana, Herero and Kgalagari life styles. All are predominantly pastoralist and each group has some commercial farmers. Those in the east, whether Afrikaner or Tswana, are in each instance more commercialised than

138

others to the north or west, who are further from markets and the attendant agencies of change. Adaptation to the common environment has led to similarities in housing, diet and recreation. Afrikaner diet at Ghanzi – goat, game, maize meal and milk – stands closer to local black practice than to European standards. Bushmen, who have a very different life style, remain effectively outside the democratic political system despite their entitlement to uniform participation.[5]

There is a wide consensus about governmental norms. Differences of opinion as to the appropriate strength of traditional as against newer instruments of local authority are contained within tribes rather than constituting issues between them. Afrikaners, too few to affect the vote, were in 1973 in effect represented in the Assembly, since one of the four seats in the gift of the legislature itself was held by a Ghanzi farmer (as it had been since 1966). However, in 1976 he was not re-elected by the legislature. Some observers have suggested that the Ghanzi Afrikaner community feels too secure to require this token any longer.

Botswana presents a contradictory picture of the legitimacy of pluralism. Non-racialism formally denies pluralism, but informally the plural framework is too entrenched to be overlooked. Ethnicity was the predominant and traditional mode of social organisation in southern Africa. Afrikaner adaptation to this pattern contrasts with the British manner in Africa, which was to proceed within the imported liberal framework developed in the industrialised West. The appropriateness of this imported framework to the southern African situation has not until very recently been seriously questioned by scholars and observers. For not only has the industrialisation of large parts of southern Africa had the consequence of making the industrial ethos increasingly appropriate to the situation, but the ethnicity of Afrikaners has, under the impact of industrialisation, been transformed in South Africa into a viciously repressive racialism. This has had the effect of damning in advance any suggestion that ethnicity might sometimes be both legitimate and appropriate. Yet political events in other African states demonstrate the persisting strength of ethnicity and the political folly of policies which ignore it.

In Botswana, government faithfulness to the policy of non-racialism is occasionally carried to extremes, as in the refusal to allow collection of ethnic statistics in the census, despite the acutely experienced need of the administration to know how many Bushmen there were in the Kalahari.[6] Recently, however, there seem to have been some concessions to ethnic interests. A Bushman Development Officer was appointed in 1974 and plans are being implemented to facilitate the transformation of Bushmen into settled pastoralists, through schemes where participation is determined by ethnic and racial criteria (Childers 1976).

139

Despite elite dedication to the philosophy of universalism, popular encapsulation in and support for the particularism of ethnicity is unquestionably strong. Tribalism comes under constant attack from the government (*Botswana Daily News*, 27 September 1973). Grass-roots support for non-racialism is generated more by the repudiation of white racialism than by any more positive ideological commitment. Botswana's citizens, heavily engaged in employment in South Africa,[7] are peculiarly exposed to white racialism in that country.

Incipient support for positive discrimination in favour of blacks in Botswana has already shown itself. The government's localisation programme is popularly seen as Africanisation by another name. There is a tendency to regard all whites as possessing citizenship rights elsewhere and a consequent reluctance to make concessions. Despite these pressures the government clearly affirms the equal rights of all citizens. In their allocation of new freehold farms on the Western State Lands, for instance, white Afrikaners have been generously favoured alongside black locals.[8]

Racial antipathies are present but muted. Sensitivity to racialism has been shaped in the colonial era; it is white racialism which is the bogy. The law which makes public expression of racial insult an offence has thus far been evoked only against whites. The legitimacy though not the legality of black hostility to whites is widely affirmed. Afrikaners, above other whites, are the enemy from whose imperial ambitions the Tswana were saved by the British. In the euphoria of Independence there has been some inevitable reaction against Britons also, leaving a wave of preferred American, Scandinavian and other volunteers.

The technical and scientific level of all Botswana citizens is uniformly low, with expertise firmly in the hands of expatriates.[9] Unlike English settlers elsewhere, Afrikaner immigrants to Bechuanaland brought very little new technology with them. Their participation in formal education parallels that of the Tswana, though adult literacy is probably higher than the national average. The Bushmen are technologically backward in the Western sense, though their techniques have hitherto proved adequate to their environment.

Cross-cutting cleavages are the final proposed safeguard for democratic pluralism; ethnicity should not coincide with differences of language, religion, political party or class. Both tribal divisions amongst the Tswana and the ethnic pluralism of the constituent tribes minimise the probability of monolithic Tswana domination. Even Afrikaans is not the exclusive possession of one group, but is shared with Coloureds and is quite widely spoken by blacks. We have little information on religious affiliation in Botswana. The major Christian denominations in Gaborone all have multi-ethnic congregations. The ruling Botswana Democratic

Party enjoys support from all groups, though opposition parties seem to be more narrowly recruited. The ethnic correlates of social class would seem to be low. Adopting a Marxist definition of class we would characterise Botswana as having a predominantly precapitalist economic structure,[10] partly proletarianised in migrant labour both to South Africa and to new mining operations within Botswana itself, which depend heavily on imported capital.[11] Small commercial capitalist entrepreneurs are emerging in all ethnic groups in response to new export marketing opportunities. A new scramble for land is afoot as entrepreneurs vie with each other for control of this valuable resource. The head start of whites in the ownership of freehold land may be set against the effective control of tribal lands by tribally powerful black producers of cattle. Government non-racialism has tended thus far to hold the ethnic balance in land control constant, though the effects of the newest policy for the enclosure and alienation of tribal lands to an economic elite have yet to be seen.[12]

Democratic pluralism in Botswana rests on the interaction of contradictory forces. The official policy of the government, universalistic non-racialism, has laid down unequivocal principles of legal equality, and has established common citizenship rights. The tempting pursuit of more thorough policies of centralisation within a single party structure has doubtless been inhibited, not only by the democratic convictions of the modernisers with their liberal emphasis on the legitimacy of and indeed the necessity for diversity, but also by the reality which faces them: the *de facto* pluralism remains a lively check against any impulse to discount ethnic realities at the grass roots. The conflicts which ensue are not inter-ethnic, but rather between modernisers at the centre and traditionalists on the periphery. Traditional institutions frequently come under fire from the governing elite whose own gain from the diminution of tribal powers is obscured by the rhetoric of development, legitimated by the endorsement of disinterested experts and international advisers whose dedication to progress has been nurtured in other contexts.

The official illegality of ethnicity confronts its informal legitimacy. The sparse population, the uniform level of accumulation, the availability of land, have thus far stilled in the popular mind the dangers of domination by one ethnic section of the nation. Economic development has not yet thrown the population into competition for scarce resources, with all its potential for ethnic manipulation. It is this future contingency which non-racialism should avert. One of the tests of the integrity of government policy will be the treatment of Afrikaners, the ability to resist the appeal of anti-white racialism, the capacity to tolerate even Afrikaner economic success.

Meanwhile the international political sympathy for liberalism declines.

141

Fig. 20. Shelling *maramas*: A Bushman woman working in the farm garden

Strident black demands for separate consideration are mutely, guiltily, conceded in the metropolitan West, where vested white power is too firmly entrenched for black power to be more than a patronised slogan. It remains to be seen how long Botswana will be able to champion a policy no longer seen as unquestionably morally right abroad, and never really understood at home, except, perhaps reluctantly, by the Afrikaners.

Long-term Afrikaner reaction to the changed political and economic circumstances of Independence is a matter of speculation. The culture of the Kalahari boers, forged in elementary physical need, is a culture if not of poverty, then certainly not of surplus. The economic prospects for commercial cattle ranching seem to promise wealth in the future. Progressive anglicisation and liberalism, in conformity to the culture of the elite, would be one way in which Afrikaners might assure their future. In the short term their response is a cautious piecemeal capitulation to particular selected pressures. It is above all still a collective response, reached in the rounds of visits to one anothers' houses, over cups of tea, sweet biscuits and slivers of *biltong* around the dining table.

'Ai yai!' sighs an Afrikaner woman, echoing the indigenous lament, as she looks from her *stoep* to the grove of dark green citrus trees beneath which two Bushman women sit shelling *marama* nuts for the coming months' baking. One of her sons is a schoolteacher in South Africa, one of her daughters has married a stock inspector in Namibia. Two of her children have married locally and ranch cattle in Ghanzi. One of her children married an Indian and lives abroad, and has not written to her for eighteen months. The cattle prices are rising, the Bushmen are asking for higher wages, the pump on the borehole needs repairing; the Bushmen say the wildebeest have broken the fences again at the cattle post. Her son is three days late in returning through the Kalahari from the Lobatse abattoir in his cattle truck.

'Ai yai! Now yes, tell them that we live well in the land under the Botswanas. We can't complain. So far we live well.'

Notes

Chapter 1. The mundane Kalahari

1. There are exceptions: see A. Kuper (1970) for an account of the Kgalagari. Silberbauer (1965) has a lucid chapter on the farms.
2. See Thomas (1969:35, 44) for Ghanzi farmer Theunis Berger's role in one research expedition. A more villainous caricature of farmers is contained in her first chapter.
3. This quotation, like others which follow unacknowledged in the text, is from the transcript of conversations recorded in the Kalahari in 1973, during six months' fieldwork supported by the Social Science Research Council (U.K.) and the British Academy.
4. 'Dutch medicine' is big business in South Africa. Lennon Ltd of Port Elizabeth, mass producers of traditional remedies, publish and distribute free a forty-eight page *Dutch medicine handbook: home remedies*, listing seventy-six preparations and their applications and indications. *Rooipoeier*: 'Hyd. Sulph. rub., Pot. Sulph., Pot. Nit. . . . useful in minor kidney and bladder complaints. A quarter of a teaspoon in water may be taken two or three times a day' (p. 23). *Hoffmansdruppels*: '90% Alcohol., 33 ml Ether . . . known and used for at least 300 years' is recommended for 'fainting, for asthma, for tightness of the chest, for colds, chills and fevers and for stomach pains . . . half a teaspoonful in a wineglassful of water' (p. 20).
5. There are seven groups of Bushmen on the Ghanzi farms. Nharo, Tsau and ≠kaba, whose languages are very closely related, predominate, and comprise almost three-quarters of the local Bushman population, followed by G/wi and G//ana who are a fifth of the population, with small numbers of Makoko (also known as ≠Au//ein or southern !Kung) and !Ko or !Xo. See Barnard (1975).
6. Details from Ghanzi commonage survey (1972).
7. The *Population census 1971* reported that 41 per cent of all Botswana's rural households did not hold any cattle (table 37). The more recent *Rural income distribution survey 1974/75* reported that 45 per cent of households own no cattle (p. 110).
8. One morgen is 0.85 square metres or 'about two acres in Holland and Dutch colonies . . . believed to be the same word as *morgen*, morn, with the sense

145

"area of land that can be ploughed in one morning"' (*Oxford English Dictionary*).

9. Tshekedi Khama, addressing the Joint Advisory Council in Lobatse in 1958, referred to the 'pressing problem of national unity as against the racial unities the citizens'. He contrasted the 'racial harmony' of Bechuanaland with the policies operating on its borders; the 'dual standards' policy of South Africa, the 'partnership' of Rhodesia, and the 'black man's country formula further afield'. He said, 'None of these principles is making smooth progress, nor do they seem to improve the tempo of racial harmony.' See *Minutes of the Joint Advisory Council* (April 1958).

Chapter 2. Boers, trekboers and *bywoners*

1. Both the physical and cultural adaptation of the Kalahari Bushmen to their environment throws doubt on the view that they were forced into the dry lands by Bantu migrants.
2. *Cape Colonial Blue Book on Native Affairs* (1897), p. 132, quoted in a letter to the Marquis of Ripon, Downing Street. BNA HC 119.
3. Letter from Major Gould Adams, near Ghanzi, to Resident Commissioner, 5 June 1896. BNA HC 140/6.
4. Enclosure from Lieutenant Walsh, Resident Magistrate Lake Ngami, to Commanding Officer Vryburg, 18 October 1894. BNA HC 144.
5. *De Britische Z. Afrikaansche Maatsch* (1894). BNA S 156/13.
6. Sir Henry Loch to Colonal Frederick Cassington, 1 May 1891, refers to the 'threatened boer trek which is being organised in the Transvaal with the avowed intention of establishing a republic'. BNA HC 87/48.
7. Undated press cutting enclosed in documents addressed to Sir Henry Loch, 1894. BNA HC 159/3.
8. Memo of conversation held at Umtali, 22 November 1897, between the High Commissioner A. Milner and C. J. Rhodes with reference to the Ngami trek. BNA HC 147.
9. The British South Africa Company undertook to bear the cost of outfitting, one half of which was to be repaid at the end of five years. See Major Gould Adams to High Commissioner Cape Town, 23 May 1898. BNA HC 49/7.
10. High Commissioner's despatch to Colonial Office, 103G, 1 June 1895. BNA HC 144.
11. Notes on the interview of the High Commissioner with the Ngami trekkers at Martisani (*sic*) siding on 28 October 1897. BNA S 156/12.
12. Major Panzera, Special Commissioner Ngamiland, Ghanzi, to Resident Commissioner, 31 October 1898. BNA RC 4/3.
13. Quit rent is a form of land purchase whereby freehold title is acquired through regular payments over a stipulated number of years.
14. Major Panzera, Ghanzi, to Resident Commissioner, 31 October 1898. BNA RC 4/3.
15. High Commissioner Johannesburg, to Resident Commissioner Mafeking, 14 March 1904. BNA RC 10/18.

16. Notes on the interview of the High Commissioner with the Ngami trekkers at Martisani (*sic*) siding on 28 October 1897. BNA s 156/12.
17. See petition to Lord Selbourne from persons of Narogas, 1910. BNA s 41/1.
18. Letter from Reverend A. Stewart, Upington, Cape, to Resident Commissioner, 6 April 1914. BNA s 4/1.
19. See Stigand's map of 1922, Land Survey Office, Gaborone; see also petition of farmers and residents of Ghanzi to His Excellency the Governor General of South Africa, Ghansisland, January 1920. BNA s 2/6.
20. In 1959 the conditions governing the sale of farms in Ghanzi stipulated for each farm 'one dwelling' and 'additional suitable accommodation for farm labour' (files of the Ministry of Agriculture 1959–60: The sale of Ghanzi farms). The terminology has changed but neither the intention nor the perception.
21. Petition of farmers and residents of Ghanzi to His Excellency the Governor General of South Africa, Ghansisland, January 1920. BNA s 2/6.
22. *Ibid*.
23. Fernleigh: report on the agricultural and pastoral possibilities of Ghansi District in Ngamiland, Palapye Road, 23 May 1913. BNA s 156/13. Exactly the same complaint recurred fifty years later in respect of the Kgalagari pastoralists of the western Kalahari. See SIDA (1972).
24. Letter from Hannay, Tsau, 19 December 1909. BNA s 42/8. By the late 1920s Afrikaners, stimulated by the Batawana example, were beginning to envisage regular commercial trans-Kalahari cattle treks.
25. Fernleigh: report on the agricultural and pastoral possibilities of Ghansi District in Ngamiland, Palapye Road, 23 May 1913. BNA s 156/13.
26. Lions are becoming more common. Night trekking has become dangerous and has been discontinued.
27. Report of the Acting Magistrate Ghanzi, 29 September 1920. BNA s 156/13.
28. Resident Magistrate Maun to Government Secretary Mafeking, 21 July 1933. BNA s 343/11.
29. Report of the Resident Magistrate Ngamiland, 26 May 1934. BNA s 395/8.

Chapter 3. Into the cash economy

1. *Minutes of the European Advisory Council* (1945).
2. The *Ghanzi District colonial annual report* (1956) reported 'a record year for cream, being an increase of nearly 2000 lbs over 11 000 lbs the previous year'. BNA s 564/12.
3. *Minutes of the European Advisory Council* (1947).
4. District Commissioner Ghanzi, report to successor, 1957. BNA s 119/3.
5. District Commissioner Ghanzi to Government Secretary, 25 October 1961. BNA s 119/3/2.
6. District Commissioner Ghanzi, report to successor, 1957. BNA s 119/3.
7. District Commissioner Ghanzi to Government Secretary, 12 February 1954. BNA s 119/3.
8. District Commissioner's report, Ghanzi, March 1956. BNA s 119/3.

9. *Minutes of the European Advisory Council* (1954).
10. *Ghanzi District colonial annual report* (1958). BNA s 539/6.
11. Report of an interview with the Ghanzi School principal, *Rand Daily Mail* (1963). Undated cutting from collection of a resident of Ghanzi.
12. Petition of residents of Ghanzi for the removal of Africans, Coloureds and poor whites, 1954. BNA s 463/3.
13. Letter from A. A. Gericke, attorney, Mafeking, accompanying the Petition (*ibid.*), 13 January 1954. BNA s 463/3.
14. Minutes of the third annual meeting of the Ghanzi Farmers' and Cattle Owners' Association, 1954. BNA s 463/3 no. 8306/6.
15. District Commissioner Ghanzi to Government Secretary, 12 February 1954. BNA s 463/3. A probable explanation is that the community were aware of the impending economic reforms, and that they were demonstrating that, whatever else they might be, they were not themselves poor whites.
16. District Commissioner Ghanzi to Government Secretary, 2 December 1953. BNA s 463/3.
17. District Commissioner Ghanzi to Government Secretary, 12 February 1954. BNA s 463/3.
18. T. Hardbattle, Buitsavango, Ghanzi to District Commissioner Ghanzi, 24 November 1953. BNA s 463/3.
19. District Commissioner Ghanzi to Government Secretary, memor Q/3, 3 December 1953. BNA s 463/3.
20. Telegram from District Commissioner Ghanzi to Divisional Commissioner, 9 February 1954. BNA s 463/3.
21. R. P. Fawcus, Mafeking to District Commissioner Maun, 16 June 1954. BNA s 463/3.
22. District Commissioner Ghazi to Government Secretary, memo Q/3, 3 December 1953. BNA s 463/3.
23. District Commissioner Ghanzi to Government Secretary, 14 May 1955. BNA s 539/6.
24. Russell England addressing the European Advisory Council, 1955. See *Minutes of the European Advisory Council* (1955).
25. Divisional Commissioner Francistown to T. E. Lawrence, Mafeking, 2 March 1954. BNA s 463/3.
26. Files of the Ministry of Agriculture, Gaborone, ref. 11737/K5, 23 November 1959.
27. *Die Burger* (Cape Town), 21 December 1961.
28. Editorial in *Die Brandende Doringbos* (Windhoek), June 1961.
29. *Die Suid Wester* (Windhoek), 11 November 1961.
30. *Rand Daily Mail* (Johannesburg), June 1965. Undated cutting from collection of a resident of Ghanzi.
31. *Mafeking Mail and Botswana Guardian*, 14 October 1966.
32. Files of Ministry of Agriculture, Gaborone, ref. 23/4/2, 14 April 1972.
33. *Minutes of European Advisory Council* (1947); also *Ghanzi District colonial annual report* (1956). BNA s 564/12.
34. Estimate of the Central Statistical Office, Gaborone, 1972.

Chapter 4. A domestic description

1. Under British rule Xanagas became the officially sanctioned place for Coloured farmers, recognition that it had long been occupied by Coloureds. Twenty-three farms at Xanagas were offered to local Coloured residents for purchase in 1960. Since 1964 racially exclusive access to land in this farming block has been dropped in accordance with government policy. The close kinship ties between the people of Xanagas and Ghanzi have dictated their common treatment in this study.

2. The racial and ethnic composition of the population is not known exactly; the non-racial policy of the government has precluded racial categorisation of the population since 1964. The 1964 figures must, however, be treated with all the caution due to the statistics of a widely dispersed non-industrial and largely illiterate population. Despite the superficial incompatibility with the 1971 census count of total population, the government in 1976 worked with an estimate of 4000 Bushmen on the Ghanzi farms (see Botswana Government Project memorandum/Ghanzi farms Basarwa Settlement scheme, 1976). This figure of 4000 was suggested by Silberbauer (1965). Much of the uncertainty is due to the seasonal migration of Bushmen from farms to veld.

3. D. F. du Toit, Kgoutsa, to H. Tumbrill, Inspector of Education, Mafeking, 1 September 1931. BNA s 89/18.

4. For example *marsyne* not *medisyne*; *soas* not *soos*; *assamblief* not *asseblief*; *og* instead of *ook* (Kemp 1920:81–7).

5. In 1973 whites paid ten rand for a general hunting licence, which gave them the right to two springbok, two wildebeest, one hartebeest, one duiker, one steenbok and four impala. Black villagers paid three rand for the same rights. A lion licence is one hundred rand for whites, ten rand for blacks, and excludes in both cases the right to the skin. In hunting areas 29 and 30 (all hunting areas in Botswana are numbered) blacks may hunt free, white citizens pay ten rand a week, and non-citizens two hundred rand a week (information from Ghanzi resident).

Chapter 5. Preserving boundaries

1. *Kom Handhaaf Saam*, ATKV (SAS and H) (*circa* 1930).

    Every person tells another person what he is the moment he talks. But still more. When he talks he reveals to another what he thinks of his own people, his heritage, himself. . . . For every people language is a priceless possession without which there would not be a people. The Afrikaners are a small people, and everyone that bears the name Afrikaner is essential to the development of the Afrikaans language. . . . Wherever we work or go to school, however rich or poor we may be, every one of us has a stake in the importance of our language and thus also in the importance of ourselves.

    There follow fifteen hints, including

    At all times speak good Afrikaans, especially to non-Afrikaners and

149

non-whites. . . . If you address a stranger or go into a shop or public place, speak Afrikaans. . . . Do not be apologetic. It is your right to be served in your own language. Approach the trader and say to him politely that you will have to take your custom elsewhere. . . . If you are in company where one or more non-Afrikaners is present do not speak English out of so-called courtesy. It is the complaint of many English-speaking people that they do not speak Afrikaans because they do not have sufficient opportunity to hear it.

2. A District Commissioner in the 1960s warned his successor, 'They are all bound together by ties of blood and marriage, and these ties have created feuds about which you will learn in due course.' BNA s 119/3/2.

3. Taljaard, Kotze, Taljaard and van Heerden, D'Kar, to Resident Commissioner Mafeking, March 1934. BNA s 89/8.

4. D. F. du Toit, Kgoutsa School, to Sergeant Brooks, Chairman Ghanzi School Committee, 23 January 1934. BNA s 89/8.

5. Report of speech by Resident Magistrate Maun to a meeting of farmers in Ghanzi, 24 May 1934. BNA s 395/8.

6. D. F. du Toit, Kgoutsa School, to Sergeant Brooks, Chairman Ghanzi School Committee, 23 January 1934. BNA s 89/8. The references to 'schoolmaster' are possibly misleading. Literacy was not highly valued, nor was teaching. In 1908 the Justice of the Peace at Wakkerstroom, giving evidence before the Transvaal Indigency Commission, listed 'keeping school as tutors with other farmers or holding school at their own houses' as one of the avenues open to the 'indigent', along with, for example, 'ploughing for kaffirs'.

7. D. F. du Toit, Kgoutsa to Tumbrill, Inspector of Education, Mafeking, 15 September 1931. BNA s 89/18.

8. Statement from T. Hardbattle, Buitsavango, recording how Africans and Coloureds came to Ghanzi. Enclosure in letter from Gericke, Mafeking, to Government Secretary, 13 January 1954. BNA s 463/3.

9. Report on D'Kar School by Mr Geyer, schoolteacher, 1 April 1951. BNA s 89/8.

10. Report of the Select Committee on Racial Discrimination (1963).

11. The meeting was fully covered in a November 1963 issue of *Die Suid-Wester* (undated press cutting from collection of a Ghanzi resident). This simultaneous fear of racial integration and racial conflagration had been noted by L. Kuper *et al.* (1958).

12. Debate on the proposal that more land be made available to European settlers. *Minutes of the European Advisory Council* (March 1954).

13. BNA s 119/3/2. The date has been omitted to preserve the anonymity of the official.

14. The issue of the transfer of at least the 'European Blocks' of the Protectorate to South Africa was a frequent one. In memorably dramatic language Glover in 1945 had predicted a Labour Party victory in Britain and the universal franchise in Bechuanaland.

The present is prosperous, but droughts, quarantines, embargoes and depressions will follow as sure as night the day, with no expansion possible for Europeans. Our farms will in time become smaller and our people poorer, with imperial grants for Africans only and state-aided schools run on non-racial lines. We are heading for racial absorption and that most cruel of all colour bars, the bar sinister of high caste. I am no racialist. I would have no objection to a couple of dozen Africans attending college with a couple of hundred European students, but where a few hundred European children will have to mix in school with a few hundred African scholars the case is totally different. . . . In our case the solution is simple. The transfer of our settlement to the Union of South Africa.

Minutes of the European Advisory Council (March 1945).

15. Nevertheless the integration of the Xanagas school was accomplished in 1964 with little public fuss. There are now more Bushmen than Coloureds in the school. The first Bushmen were admitted in 1969. A Coloured woman whose children were at the school said of the Bushmen, 'Soon they'll be the masters and we'll be working for them', and added with a happy sigh, 'But I'll be dead by then.'

Chapter 6. Boers and Bushmen

1. Notes on the interview of the High Commissioner with the Ngami trekkers at Martisani (*sic*) siding on 28 October 1897. BNA s 156/12.
2. Not so the Batawana from Ngamiland. See Tlou (1972).
3. Captain Fuller, Kgoutsa, to Newton, 8 May 1895. Enclosure in High Commissioner's despatch to Colonial Office, 103G, 1 June 1895. BNA HC 144.
4. Petition of settlers to Resident Commissioner, 23 April 1910. BNA s 156/3.
5. Botswana Government Project memorandum/Ghanzi farms Basarwa Settlement scheme (1976).
6. Reverend Wookey, Molepolole, to Sidney Shippard, Administrator Bechuanaland Protectorate, 21 July 1894. BNA HC 153/1.
7. Resident Magistrate, Taung, to Sidney Shippard, Administrator Bechuanaland Protectorate, 16 April 1887. BNA HC 153/1.
8. *The Masarwa (Bushmen) report, London Missionary Society* (1935).
9. Comment on the Masarwa census by District Commissioner Serowe, 3 October 1936.
10. Resident Commissioner Ngamiland to High Commissioner Johannesburg, 10 July 1906. BNA s 7.
11. In Ghanzi in 1964 Afrikaners challenged local Bushmen to an archery competition; the Bushman defeat was triumphantly reported in the *Mafeking Mail*. Afrikaners confess that they were 'dead lucky that day'.
12. The petition of farmers and residents of Ghanzi to His Excellency the Governor General of South Africa, Ghansisland, January 1920, complains of 'wild Bushmen who are constantly marauding, setting fire to our grass, stealing and slaughtering our stock'. BNA s 2/6.
13. A rather different practice prevailed in Namibia. An Afrikaner immigrant from South West recollected an expedition in the 1940s following for two

days the *spoor* (tracks) of Bushmen workers who had suddenly absented themselves.

14. On a company farm in Ghanzi in 1973 the weekly food ration per worker was fifteen measures of *mieliemeel*, measured in a 2 lb jam tin, 5 lb sugar, $\frac{1}{2}$ lb coffee, $\frac{1}{2}$ lb tobacco. Meat was an occasional extra. Cash payment on this farm ranged from five to twelve rands monthly. A government survey in 1975 found average Bushman cash wages (excluding payment in kind or its cash equivalent) to be R6.4 (Botswana Government Project memorandum/Ghanzi farms Basarwa Settlement scheme, 1976).

15. Botswana Government Project memorandum Ghanzi farms Basarwa Settlement scheme (1976). These figures accord with those of the Ghanzi labour inspection report, 1971, which reported an average of seventeen employees per farming establishment. When allowance is made for farm size this is 4.2 employees per 5000 morgen.

16. Calculations are based on figures from the Botswana Government Project memorandum/Ghanzi farms Basarwa Settlement scheme (1976), pp. 4 and 7. Applying the ratio of workers to dependants given on p. 4. to the 'unwanted squatters', we calculate a potential working population of 990, of whom 68 per cent are employed by farmers. The 56 per cent of Bushmen who rejected the option of quitting the farms were presumably all employed. The 44 per cent who wanted to quit presumably included the estimated 32 per cent unemployed.

17. A petition to the Resident Commissioner, delivered at a meeting in Ghanzi on 21 July 1937 and signed by thirteen farmers, asked for the 'removal of native farmers to more than thirty or forty miles from the nearest Ghanzi farm'. The reference was to Damara and Baralong farmers. In 1944 the Ghanzi representative on the European Advisory Board moved that 'Hottentots be not allowed to migrate and settle at Olifantskloof in the Ghanzi District' (*Minutes of the European Advisory Council*, 1944). In 1954 Ghanzi residents petitioned for the removal of all non-Europeans 'with only one exception ... the Bushmen'. BNA s 463/3. See also chapter 8.

18. The attempt to establish time is even more unsatisfactory. 'Where were you on 5 June?' elicits a non-comprehending shrug from a Bushman witness. When rephrased impatiently as, 'Where were you sometime in June?', the question becomes the appropriate cue for the witness to plunge voluntarily into incriminating evidence.

Chapter 7. Sharing religion

1. Numbers did increase, however. Peak membership was reached in 1961 when there were 168 members. By 1965 numbers had fallen to 91 (information supplied by local church officers, 1973).

2. This is the decisive characteristic distinguishing 'historic' from 'archaic' religion in Bellah's typology (1964).

3. Statements of agonising doubt about the validity of conversions abound in

missionary records. See for example *Proceedings of the South India Missionary Conference held at Ootacamund* (1858).

4. J. Philip described the missionaries' task as 'locating the savages among whom they labour, teaching them industrious habits, creating a demand for British manufactures and increasing their dependence on the Colony'. He concluded that 'missionary stations are the most effective agents which can be employed to promote the internal strength of our colonies and the cheapest and best military posts a government can employ' (1828:227).

5. *The Churchman* (January 1975).

6. Letter from Church Boards and Congregation, Oranje Vrijstaat, to de Cock, 1857. Cited by Pont (1959).

Chapter 8. Boers, bureaucrats and blacks

1. *Report of the Transvaal Indigency Commission 1906–8*, Para 210, Q 5313, evidence of Andrew McKechnie.

2. Fernleigh: report on the agricultural and pastoral possibilities of the Ghansi District in Ngamiland, Palapye Road, 23 May 1913. BNA s 156/13.

3. Report of the Acting Resident Magistrate Ghanzi to Resident Commissioner Mafeking, 7 June 1934. BNA s 395/9.

4. *Report of the Transvaal Indigency Commission 1906–8*, para. 127.

5. District Commissioner's report to successor, Ghanzi, 19 January 1939. BNA s 119/3/1.

6. Resident Magistrate Ghanzi to Resident Commissioner Mafeking, 7 June 1934. BNA s 395/9.

7. Colonel Rey to Resident Magistrate Maun, 20 June 1934. BNA s 395/9.

8. District Commissioner's comments on petition of Ghanzi residents, 1954. BNA s 463/3.

9. We are grateful to the Botswana Government for access to confidential files which shed much light on the last phase of Protectorate rule. As a matter of discretion we have omitted from the text and notes such detail as readily identifies the authors, though we give the archival reference. BNA s 119/3/2.

10. The administration were under constant pressure to reduce or waive the rental of £5. See *Minutes of the European Advisory Council* (1943).

11. The recommendation that farms be surveyed came from the Gaitskell Mission on the possibility of development in the western Kalahari, 1953–4. See *Minutes of the European Advisory Council* (1954). The issue of the inability of Ghanzi leaseholders to raise a bond was discussed in special session of the European Advisory Council, 16–17 April 1956. See the confidential minutes of the European Advisory Council (1956).

12. District Commissioner to Divisional Commissioner, 4 January 1958. BNA NPA 3.

13. In December 1959 successful applicants for farms were informed of the farm they had been allocated, and of the price, which they were invited to pay over fifteen years (extended on 24 September 1964 to twenty-five years). Non-locals had five years to complete purchase. Intending buyers who were not

citizens had to make full payment immediately. Files of the Ministry of Agriculture, Gaborone, ref. 11737/к5, 23 November 1959.

14. The close confines of the Ghanzi world are reflected in the sponsors cited in applications. 81 per cent of these were other local farmers.
15. No more than two adult European males were allowed on each farm.
16. Not always with the integrity that might have been expected. In 1970 the Land Settlement Officer absconded with farmers' rents, abandoning the three farms which he had allocated to his own private company.
17. Files of the Ministry of Agriculture, ref. 11737/к5, 23 November 1959.
18. Farm 80 reverted to the state on 8 October 1964. Pressure to withdraw the forfeiture clause came from entrepreneurs who still found themselves unable to raise loans on such insecure terms.
19. Government Secretary to District Commissioner Ghanzi, 8 August 1936.
20. Resident Magistrate Ghanzi to Government Secretary, 22 August 1936.
21. J. C. Lewis, Kgoutsa, to Resident Magistrate Ghanzi, 24 July 1936.
22. Petition delivered to Resident Commissioner at a meeting of the Ghanzi farmers, Ghanzi, 21 July 1937.
23. District Commissioner Ghanzi to Government Secretary, 18 May 1936.
24. *The Observer Colour Supplement* (4 September 1976) carried a colour photograph of a similar contraption in Botswana, driven by blacks.
25. The Central Statistical Office, Gaborone, has estimated that there were 350 freehold farmers in Botswana in 1972. From an examination of surnames it would seem that some 300 of these are of Afrikaner origin.
26. In 1960 the successful applicants for freehold land each had an average of 387 head of cattle, a figure which was probably inflated by their wish to magnify their capital resources at the time of their application. In 1971 the average cattle holding as reflected in income tax returns was 1446, probably an underestimate to avoid taxation. However, there are great variations in wealth still. 90 per cent of all Ghanzi farming units have an average stock value of R9205 as compared with R234 528 for the top 10 per cent (income tax returns for 1972).
27. For an account of the District Council and its very different importance to local blacks see A. Kuper (1970:49–60).

Chapter 9. Whites in a black state

1. In 1969 the United States of America reverted to the practice of including questions on ethnic origin in the census. In 1964 Botswana, then the Bechuanaland Protectorate, suspended the ethnic enumeration in the census.
2. Something of the ethnic heterogeneity of the political unit, the tribe, is conveyed in the following: 'the modern Ngwato tribe contains communities of Kaa, Phaleng, Pedi, Tswapong, Kurutshe, Birwa, Kalaka, Taloate, Herero, Kwena, Nabye, Rotse, Subia, Kgalagadi and Sarwa'. Schapera notes 'the Ngwato proper' enjoy high rank and social prestige within this heterogeneous community 'by virtue of their origin' (Schapera 1938:4, 30–1).

154

3. See the enquiry into alleged racial discrimination at the Lobatse abattoir (1967) for an account of popular black misconceptions that 'localisation' in Botswana meant the replacement of whites by blacks.
4. Approximately 3 per cent of the registered voters in the farming block are Afrikaners, representing half of the eligible whites (see table 4).

TABLE 4. *Numbers on Electoral Roll, Ghanzi, 1973*

Electoral area*	Total on roll	Estimated number of whites on roll
South-western farms (including Camp)	1048	21
North-western farms (Farm 69)	237	26
North-eastern farms (Farm 81)	328	9
D'Kar	295	9
TOTAL	1908 (or 58% of the eligible population)†	65 (or 2.9% of the registered voters)

* The boundaries of the census enumeration areas do not coincide with electoral area boundaries, hence the discrepancy with table 3.

† 36% of the Ghanzi population is estimated to be under twenty-one years of age. There are thus some 3270 adults eligible for the electoral roll. Bushmen, while under-registered, are 80% of the Ghanzi farming block population and must constitute the bulk of the voters.

5. Bushmen are probably the majority on the voters' roll in the farming block by virtue of their sheer numerical preponderance. But they are reputedly apathetic at elections. There have never been any Bushman candidates. However, for an account that suggests their rising political consciousness see Guenther (1975).
6. In 1974 the Central Statistical Office systematically solicited estimates of the size of the Bushman population from all specialists known to have had recent experience of the Kalahari. Since then the government has sponsored surveys of the farm Bushmen. Barnard (1975), Childers (1976).
7. 25 per cent of Botswana's male population between the ages of fifteen and fifty-four is always absent, as labour in the Republic of South Africa. See *National Development Plan* (1973), diagram 1.7.
8. Between November 1966 and April 1970 thirteen farms changed hands by private treaty, eight to white citizens, four to black citizens, one to an alien. In April 1970 the government declared eleven new farms on the state land abutting the farming block, of which seven were allocated to black and four

to white citizens. In private sales few blacks can compete with the high offers made by wealthy white speculators.

9. Expatriates, comprising only 4.2 per cent of the population who have left school, comprise 61.8 per cent of all those with higher education in Botswana. Calculation based on *Population Census 1971*, table 19.

10. Though this is to take a naive and ethnocentric view of tribal capital as non-capital.

11. Diamonds were discovered at Orapa in 1967. Production started in 1971 financed by de Beers (Anglo-American), with Botswana Government holding 50 per cent of shares and receiving an estimated 65–70 per cent of the profits. Diamonds are now the largest component in exports. Copper mining at Selebi-Pikwe started in 1973, but by 1975 had not proved profitable. Roan Selection Trust, holding 85 per cent of shares, reported R20 million loss for the first half of 1975. These two mining projects provide 4500 jobs. Miners have already been on strike demanding South African wage rates. Jones (1976).

12. Botswana's adoption in 1974 of a policy of enclosure of common land by the wealthiest cattle owners was supported by the rhetoric of development, progress and pasture conservation. See Chambers and Feldman (1972) and subsequent Government White Paper of 1973. The Central Statistical Office, Gaborone, calculated that only two hundred non-freeholding households in Botswana will qualify for rights to the enclosed land, since only two hundred own more than the stipulated minimum of four hundred cattle. *Rural income distribution survey 1974/75* (1976), p. 112.

Bibliography

1. Sources, by author

Adam, Heribert. 1971. *Modernising racial domination*. London: University of California Press.

Adorno, T. W., E. Frenkel-Brunswick, D. J. Levinson, and R. N. Sandford. 1951. *The authoritarian personality*. New York: Harper & Brothers.

Allen, Sheila. 1971. *New minorities, old conflicts: Asian and West Indian migrants in Britain*. New York: Random House.

Andersson, C. J. 1857. *Lake Ngami: explorations and discoveries during four years wandering in the wilds of south western Africa*. New York.

Apter, David. 1963. 'Political religion' in C. Geertz (ed.), *Old societies and new states*. New York: Free Press.

Baines, T. 1864. *Explorations in south west Africa*. London.

Barnard, Alan. 1975. 'Report to the Ministry of Local Government and Lands on a survey of the farm Basarwa'. October (mimeo).

Barth, Frederick. 1969. *Ethnic groups and boundaries*. Bergen: Universitets Forlaget.

Bellah, R. 1964. 'Religious evolution' in R. Robertson (ed.), *Sociology of religion*. Harmondsworth: Penguin, 1970.

Berger, Peter L. 1969. *The social reality of religion*. London: Faber & Faber. First published as *The sacred canopy*. New York: Doubleday, 1967.

Bley, Helmut. 1971. *South West Africa under German rule, 1894–1914*. English version. London: Heinemann.

Bushell, Horace. 1847. 'Barbarism the first danger' in P. Rieff (ed.), *On intellectuals*. New York: Doubleday, 1969.

Chambers, John, and David Feldman. 1972. *Report on rural development in Botswana*. Gaborone: Ministry of Finance and Planning.

Childers, Gary. 1976. *Report on the survey investigation of the Ghanzi farm Basarwa situation*. Gaborone: Government Printer.

Clifford, B. E. H. 1930. 'A journey by motor lorry from Mahalapye through the Kalahari desert', *The Geographical Journal*.

Cohen, Abner (ed.). 1974. *Urban ethnicity*. ASA Monograph 12. London: Tavistock.

Bibliography

Cohen, Percy. 1966. 'Social attitudes and sociological enquiry', *British Journal of Sociology*, 17:4.

Debenham, Frank. 1953. *Kalahari sand*. London: G. Bell and Sons Ltd.

Devitt, Paul. 1974 'An addendum to the SIDA report on the village areas development project of the western State Lands of Botswana'. December 1972.

Douglas, Mary. 1966. *Purity and danger*. London: Routledge and Kegan Paul.

Durkheim, E. 1915. *Elementary forms of the religious life*. London: George Allen and Unwin.

Fishbein, Martin. 1967. 'Attitude and the prediction of behaviour' in *Readings in attitude theory and measurement*. New York: John Wiley and Sons Inc.

Geertz, Clifford. 1966. 'Religion as a cultural system' in M. Banton (ed.), *Anthropological approaches to the study of religion*. ASA Monograph 3. London: Tavistock.

Gillet, Simon. 1969. 'Notes on the settlement of the Ghanzi District', *Botswana Notes and Records* (Gaborone), 2.

Glazer, Nathan. 1975. 'The universalisation of ethnicity: peoples in a boiling pot', *Encounter*, February.

Guenther, M. G. 1975. 'The trance dancer as an agent of social change among the farm Bushmen of the Ghanzi District', *Botswana Notes and Records* (Gaborone), 7.

Heber, R. 1933. 'From Greenland's icy mountains' (hymn), *The English Hymnal*, 547.

Hill, C. S. 1963. *West Indian migrants and the London churches*. London: Oxford University Press.

Hinchliff, P. B. 1968. *The church in South Africa*. London: SPCK.

Horrell, Muriel. 1957. *A survey of race relations in South Africa 1956–1957*. Johannesburg: South African Institute of Race Relations.

Jones, David. 1976. 'Economy [of Botswana]' in *Africa south of the Sahara*. London: Europa.

Jooste, J. P. 1959. *Die geskiedenis van die Gereformeerde Kerk in Suid-Afrika 1859–1959* (The history of the Reformed church in South Africa 1859–1959). Potchefstroom.

Kemp, J. 1920. *Hoe om gesond te word en gesond te bly, natuurgeneeswyse* (How to become healthy and stay healthy, by nature healing methods). Potchefstroom.

Kuper, Adam. 1970. *Kalahari village politics*. Cambridge: Cambridge University Press.

Kuper, Adam and George Silberbauer. 1966. 'Kgalagari masters and bushman serfs', *African Studies*, 25 (April).

Kuper, Leo. 1969. 'Political change in White settler societies: the possibility of peaceful democratisation' in L. Kuper and M. G. Smith (eds.), *Pluralism in Africa*. Berkeley: University of California Press.

Kuper, Leo. 1970. 'Race structure in the social consciousness' in P. Baxter and B. Sansom (eds.), *Race and social difference*. Harmondsworth: Penguin, 1972.

Kuper, Leo, Hilstan Wats and Ronald Davies. 1958. *Durban, a study in racial ecology*. London: Cape.

MacCrone, I. D. 1965. *Race attitudes in South Africa: historical, experimental and psychological studies*. First published 1937. Johannesburg: Witwatersrand Press.

MacDonald, William. 1913. *The conquest of the desert*. London: Werner Laurie.

Malherbe, E. G. 1939. 'Report on the education of the Europeans of the Bechuanaland Protectorate'. Pretoria: National Bureau of Educational and Social Research for the Union of South Africa (mimeo).

Mehl, R. 1970. *The sociology of protestantism*. English edition. London: SCM Press.

Neill, Stephen. 1964. *A history of christian missions*. Harmondsworth: penguin.

Newcomb, Harvey. 1860. *Cyclopedia of missions*. New York: Scribner

Niebuhr, H. R. 1964. *The social sources of denominationalism*. Cleveland, Ohio: World Publications.

Passarge, S. 1905. 'Die Grundlinien im ethnographischen Bilde der Kalahari-Region' (Principles of the ethnographic picture in the Kalahari region) in *Zeitschrift der Gesellschaft für Erdkunde*. Berlin.

Passarge, S. 1907. *Die Bushmanner der Kalahari* (The Bushmen of the Kalahari). Berlin.

Pettigrew, T. F. 1960. 'Social distance attitudes of South African students', *Social Forces*, 38:3.

Philip, J. 1828. *Researches in South Africa illustrating the civil, moral and religious condition of the native tribes etc*. Vol. 2. London.

Phillips, Derek. 1973. *Abandoning method*. London: Jossey-Bass.

Pim, A. 1933. *Report by Mr. A. W. Pim on the financial and economic position of the Bechuanaland Protectorate, March 1933*. 1932–3, Cmd 4368, x, 279.

Pont, A. D. 1959. ''n ontleding van die teologiese dogmatiese agtergrond van Ds. S. D. Venter se afskeiding van die Gereformeerde Kerk in die O.V.S.' (A description of the theological and dogmatic background to Rev. S. D. Venter's break with the Reformed Church in the O.F.S.), *Hervormde Teologiese Studies*, 16.

Rubin, I. 1975. 'Ethnicity and cultural pluralism', *Phylon*, 36.

Russell, Margo. 1976. 'Slaves or workers? Relations between Bushmen, Tswana and boers in the Kalahari', *Journal of Southern African Studies*. 2:2.

Sahlins, Marshall. 1974. *Stone age economics*. London: Tavistock.

Schapera, Isaac. 1930. *The Khoisan peoples of South Africa: Bushmen and Hottentots*. London: Routledge and Sons.

Schapera, Isaac. 1938. *A handbood of Tswana law and custom*. Second edition. London: Oxford University Press, 1955.

Schapera, Isaac. 1955. *Tribal innovators: Tswana chiefs and social change 1795–1940*. London: Athlone Press.

Schapera, Isaac and J. van der Merwe. 1943. *A comparative study of Kgalagadi, Kwena and other Sotho dialects*. Communications from the School of African Studies, New Series 9, University of Cape Town.

Schapera, Isaac and J. van der Merwe. 1945. *Notes on tribal groupings, history and customs of the Bakgalagadi.* Communications from the School of African Studies, New Series 13, University of Cape Town.

SIDA. 1972. 'The village areas development project of the western State Lands of Botswana'. Findings and recommendations by a consultancy mission from the Swedish International Development Authority.

Silberbauer, George. 1965. 'Report to the government of Bechuanaland on the Bushman Survey'. Gaborone.

Sillery, A. 1952. *The Bechuanaland Protectorate.* Cape Town: Oxford University Press.

Sillery, A. 1965. *Founding a protectorate: history of Bechuanaland 1885–1895.* The Hague: Mouton and Co.

Simmel, Georg. 1964. *Conflict and the web of group affiliations.* New York: Glencoe Free press.

Stigand, A. G. 1912. 'Notes on Ngamiland', *The Geographical Journal.*

Stigand, A. G. 1923. 'Ngamiland', *The Geographical Journal,* 62:6.

Tagart, E. S. B. 1931. *Report on the Masarwa and on corporal punishment among the natives in the Bamangwato reserve of the Bechuanaland Protectorate.* Dominions 136, October.

Tajfel, Henri. 1969. 'Cognitive aspects of prejudice', *Journal of Social Issues,* 25:4.

Thomas, Elizabeth Marshall. 1969. *The harmless people.* Harmondsworth: Penguin.

Thomas, Kerry (ed.). 1971. *Attitudes and behaviour: selected readings.* Harmondsworth: Penguin.

Tlou, Thomas. 1972. 'A political history of north-western Botswana to 1906'. University of Wisconsin, unpublished Ph.D. dissertation.

van den Berghe, P. 1962. 'Race attitudes in Durban, South Africa', *Journal of Social Psychology,* 57.

van den Berghe, Pierre. 1969. 'Pluralism and the polity' in L. Kuper and M. G. Smith (eds.), *Pluralism in Africa.* Berkeley: University of California Press.

van den Berghe, Pierre. 1972. 'Distance mechanisms of stratification in A. Richmond (ed.), *Readings in race and ethnic relations.* London: Pergamon Press.

Wicker, Allan W. 1969. 'Attitudes versus actions: the relationship of verbal and overt behavioural responses to attitude objects', *Journal of Social Issues,* 25:4.

Wilson, M. and L. Thompson (eds.). 1969. *The Oxford history of South Africa.* Vol. 1. Oxford: Clarendon Press.

2. Additional sources in chronological order

Manuscripts in the Botswana National Archives (BNA), Gaborone.

Proceedings of the South India Missionary Conference held at Ootacamund, 19 April–5 May, Madras, 1858.

De Britische Z. Afrikaansche Maatsch (The British South Africa Company). Pamphlet, 1894.

Cape colonial blue book on native affairs, Q33–79, 1897.

Report of the Transvaal Indigency Commission 1906–8, TG 13/08, Pretoria, 1908

Minutes of the European Advisory Council, 1922–64.

Kom Handhaaf Saam, ATKV (SAS and H). Undated, *circa* 1930.

The Masarwa (Bushmen) report of an inquiry by the South African District Committee of the London Missionary Society, Lovedale, March 1935.

Minutes of the Ghanzi Farmers' and Cattle Owners' Association, 1954–73.

Ghanzi District colonial annual reports 1956, 1958.

Minutes of the Joint Advisory Council of the Bechuanaland Protectorate, 1958.

Report of the Select Committee on Racial Discrimination to the Legislative Council, 22 November 1963.

Enquiry into alleged racial discrimination at the Lobatse abattoir, 1967.

Ghanzi District development plan, 1969–73.

Ghanzi labour inspection report, November 1971.

Ghanzi commanage survey, Ghanzi Development Officer, 25 May 1972.

Minutes of the second meeting of the Rural Development Council, 23–28 November 1972.

Report on the population census 1971, Gaborone: Central Statistical Office, August 1972.

Rural development in Botswana, Government Paper 1, Gaborone, March 1972.

Ghanzi Development Officer's report, 1973.

National Development Plan, Part 1, Gaborone: Government Printer, July 1973.

Ghanzi Communication study: interim report, presented to the Ministry of Works and Communications, Republic of Botswana, by Messrs VIAK A/S and Hoff and Overgaard, January 1974.

Botswana Government Project memorandum/Ghanzi farms Basarwa Settlement scheme, LG 32(v), 1976.

Botswana Government Project memorandum/Land and water development for Ghanzi farms Basarwa, LG 32(v), 1976.

Rural income distribution survey 1974/75, Gaborone: Government Printer, 1976.

3. Newspapers

Botswana Daily News (Gaborone).

Die Brandende Doringbos (Windhoek).

Die Burger (Cape Town).

The Churchman (U.K.).

Mafeking Mail (Mafeking).

Mafeking Mail and Botswana Guardian (Mafeking).

The Observer (U.K.).

Rand Daily Mail (Johannesburg).

Die Suid-Wester (Windhoek).

Index

Index

165

Index

Milner, Sir Alfred, 13, 15–16, 146 n.8
missions to Bushmen, 99, 106–14
Mochudi, 11, 75
Moermoeryas, 25
Molopo, 75–6
Molopolole, 11, 13, 21, 64
Moremi II, Chief, 11

Naitsho, 80
Nama, xi, xii, 1, 16, 22, 43, 57, 58, 68, 73, 89, 90, 119
Namibia, xi, 1, 11, 24–6, 43, 49, 51, 56, 58, 68–9, 77, 95–7, 99, 107–8, 111, 115–16, 125–7, 143, 151
Nederduitse Gereformeerde church, 62–72, 99, 103–15
'new trekkers', 29–30, 123
Newcomb, H., 118–19
Ngamiland, 11, 18, 20, 21–2, 38, 58, 77, 82, 127
Ngamiland Trading Company, 4, 106, 116
Nharo Bushmen, 4, 58, 60, 68, 90, 116, 126, 145 n.5
see also Bushmen
Niebuhr, H. R., 101
non-racial policy, 3, 7–8, 35, 57, 65, 123–4, 131, 135–6, 139, 149 nn.1, 2
Nossob, 11, 58, 76
Nughae, 80

Okavango, 11–12, 24, 90, 126
Okwa, 10–11, 21
Olifantskloof, 11, 22, 23, 56
oral history, 8–9

Panzera, Major, 14–15, 29, 146 nn.12, 14
Passarge, S., 10, 79–80
Patriot, Die, 12
paternalism, 86
patronage, *see* clientship
petitions
  1910, 8, 147 n.17, 151 n.4
  1920, 17, 20, 147 n.19, 151 n.12
  1937, 124–5, 152 n.17
  1953, 32, 120, 148 n.13
Pettigrew, T., 130
Philip, J., 118–19, 153 n.4
Phillips, Derek, 130
Pim, A., 20, 22, 28
Pitsani, 11, 13
pluralism, 138–41
political participation of Afrikaners, 62, 134, 137, 155 n.4
poor whites, 32–4, 43, 47, 119–20, 122–3, 148 n.15, 154 n.26

see also bywoners
population statistics
  Afrikaners in Angola, 25
  Batawana Reserve 1921, 20
  Bushmen, 149 n.2, 152 n.16
  decline of Afrikaners in Ghanzi, 29–30, 34
  early Ghanzi settlement, 12, 14, 17
  farming block, 40–1, 48
  Ghanzi Camp, 6
  Ghanzi District 1921, 20
Portuguese, 25, 95
Pretoria, 11, 59, 59

quit rent, 14, 146 n.13

race theories in sociology, 7, 137–8
racial attitudes, *see* attitudes
racial and ethnic abuse, 33, 45, 117, 133–4
racial integration, 3, 5, 35, 57, 64–6, 68–9, 71–6, 81, 99, 106, 127, 135–7, 150 n.11, 151 n.15
racial segregation, 3, 5, 32–3, 40, 58–9, 63–5, 68–9, 70–5, 152 n.17
see also apartheid
Rakops, 11, 24
religion
  and Afrikaner identity, 62–72
  church services, 50–2, 62, 77, 107–12
  definitions of, 114–15
  denominational divisions, 62–72, 77
  and government policy, 99, 111, 114
  membership figures, 34, 99, 104, 109, 152 n.1
  missionary conflict with settlers, 71, 99–102, 106–12, 152 n.3, 153 n.4
  nagmaal, 51, 107–12
  predikant, 25, 51, 69, 105, 109
  sharing religion
    with blacks, 55, 71, 77
    with Bushmen, 51, 71, 99, 105–12
    with Coloureds, 63–4, 68–9
  sociological theories of, 100–3
  universalism of Christianity, 70, 100–3, 112, 115
  worship at home, 52, 68, 105

Sahlins, M., 84
San, xi
  see Bushmen
Schapera, I., xi, 17, 82, 93, 154 n.2
schools, *see* education
Segkobas Pan, 124
Serowe, 11, 74, 82
sex roles of Afrikaners, 54–5
sexual relations of Afrikaners

166

For EU product safety concerns, contact us at Calle de José Abascal, 56–1°,
28003 Madrid, Spain or eugpsr@cambridge.org.

www.ingramcontent.com/pod-product-compliance
Ingram Content Group UK Ltd.
Pitfield, Milton Keynes, MK11 3LW, UK
UKHW010047140625
459647UK00012BB/1671